Aloha Las Vegas

and Other Plays

EDWARD SAKAMOTO

D1195642

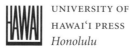

UNIVERSITY OF
HAWAI'I PRESS
Honolulu

PS
3569
.A45459
A79
2000

Published with the support of the Maurice J. Sullivan & Family Fund
of the University of Hawai'i Foundation.

Printed in the United States of America

05 04 03 02 01 00   5 4 3 2 1

Library of Congress Cataloging-in-Publication Data
Sakamoto, Edward, 1940–
    Aloha Las Vegas and other plays / Edward Sakamoto.
      p.   cm.
    Contents: A'ala Park — Stew Rice — Aloha Las Vegas.
    ISBN 0–8248–2276–5 (pbk. : alk. paper)
    1. Hawaii—Drama. I. Title.

PS3569.A45459 A79 2000
812'.54 — dc21   00–023411

University of Hawai'i Press books are printed on acid-free
paper and meet the guidelines of permanence and
durability of the Council on Library Resources.

Designed by Bonnie Campbell, Running Feet Books

Printed by Versa Press

To my aunts of the Sakamoto and Hatakeyama families:

Mrs. Tadako Yoshikawa, Mrs. Fusa Sakamoto, Mrs. Yoshiko

Sakamoto, Mrs. Kimie Kuroyama, Mrs. Doris Hatakeyama.

Contents

Acknowledgments

Through the years friends have been a source of unfailing support. To all of them, my heartfelt thanks for sticking with me on my long journey.

Marge Powers, Pauline Serritelli, and Tim Connor
Hideo and Eleanor Anzai
Jon and Barbara Shirota
Louise Sakamoto
Daniel, Marilyn, Stephanie, and Jennifer Soo
Karen Huie
Bill Shinkai
Craig Walker
Roy and Jane Asato
Geoffrey and Linda Luke
Wakako and Joy Yamauchi

Thanks also to Harry Wong III, Artistic Director, Gene Shofner, Managing Director, and Justina T. Mattos, Archivist, Kumu Kahua Theatre, Honolulu; James A. Nakamoto; Artistic Director Tisa Chang and the staff at Pan Asian Repertory, New York; Tim Dang, Producing Artistic Director, East West Players, Los Angeles; Elsa Carroll; Carol Rosegg; Corky Lee; the various photographers for their courtesy and generosity; Sharon Yamamoto, our editor at University of Hawai'i Press, for her consistent enthusiasm and help.

Introduction

Sakamoto in the Theatre:

Displaced Protagonists, Challenged Spectators

Dennis Carroll

All three plays in this collection were premiered in Hawaiʻi by Kumu Kahua Theatre, the local community theatre, established in 1971, which has as its mission the development and production of plays written by residents or set locally and that deal with Hawaiʻi. As Honolulu-born-and-raised Sakamoto has lived in California since 1966, it is something of a paradox that his nine plays set in Hawaiʻi have been the backbone of the company's repertory since 1984 and have been lauded for the authenticity of their "local" pidgin, rhythms, and atmosphere. The plays in this, his second collection have all been produced on the mainland as well, as have the plays in the earlier *Hawaiʻi No Ka Oi: The Kamiya Family Trilogy.*

The most challenging theme of Edward Sakamoto's local plays centers around the consequences of a Hawaiʻi resident's choice to relocate to the mainland and the issue of whether it is possible for the transplanted person ever to reclaim home.[1] In what follows, I will first touch on the contexts of reception of the plays in Hawaiʻi and on the mainland before going into more detail about the development, production history, and thematic orchestration of each of these plays, focusing on their key themes.

I think it is important to question any assumption that these plays are mere popular entertainment providing provenance for easy empathy and identification for local and Hawaiʻi expatriate audiences. On the surface, the local Sakamoto plays seem to invite unproblematic

1

identification and empathy because of their family-based subject matter, liberal use of pidgin comedy, artful employment of nostalgia, and, most of all, their predominantly realist form and style. But in analyzing responses to Asian American plays, Josephine Lee has noted that the use of realism in such plays need not be a simple means to promote recognition, empathy, and endorsement among Asian American or any other spectators. Lee challenges the kinds of plays, and readings of plays, that promote a "celebration of ethnic solidarity, an idealized vision of Asian American theatres full of Asian American audiences," preferring a model of spectatorship and reading that "allows for a more partial and tentative identification."[2] Arguably, this is indeed what happens to the responsive spectator at these Sakamoto plays. The unresolved questions and the lack of reassuring closure in the plays promote just this feeling of uneasy complexity rather than an uncritical empathy or affirmative recognition.

Audience reception[3] of the plays locally has been especially colored by the changing sociopolitical context of Hawaiʻi from 1984 to 1998, the period in which successive productions of these plays were offered. This changing context, I suggest, would tend to deconstruct any tendency toward unanimity of response on the part of any given audience —and more and more so with the passing of time. It would particularly problematize any positive endorsement of the nostalgic 1950s scenes and characters' reminiscences of that period, as well as spectators' empathy with the protagonists and their choices of staying in or leaving Hawaiʻi.

The most noticeable factor in the local sociopolitical context of these years was the downturn toward disenchantment: the erosion of mutual trust and a sense of unanimity of and solidarity among locals of all ethnicities.[4] Jonathan Okamura has identified some of these changes as "substantially increased investment from Japan during the latter half of the 1980's, the tremendous expansion of the tourist industry in the economy of Hawaiʻi, the continued development of the movement for Hawaiian sovereignty and for recognition of their rights and claims as the indigenous people of Hawaiʻi, and the widening social cleavage between Japanese Americans and other ethnic groups, particularly Filipino Americans, Native Hawaiians, and haole or white Americans."[5] Finally, the "Japan bubble" of inflated property values in the late 1980s, the bursting of the bubble in 1991, and the deepening recession of the later 1990s have further eroded unanimity and trust, and even the belief among locals of all ethnicities that "lucky you live Hawai'i."

A more positive aspect of this dissolution of local solidarity among the various groups has been the development of an exciting plurality in the voices heard in literary and other art forms during the same period. Spectators and readers increasingly sought more than superficial likenesses in local literature and theatre, expecting more than simplistic unanimity in characterizing what "local" was. Two landmark events in the development of these changing expectations in the later 1970s were the publication of Milton Murayama's classic *All I Asking For Is My Body* in 1975, and the foundation in 1978 of *Bamboo Ridge*, the literary periodical that was, and still is, the major forum for local fiction and poetry in Hawai'i. In 1981 Kumu Kahua separated from the University of Hawai'i at Mānoa Theatre and Dance Department as an independent community theatre, instituted regular summer statewide tours under the auspices of the State Foundation on Culture and the Arts, and developed more diversity in its choices of local plays, so that pidgin was no longer the major yardstick of a badge of ethnicity uniting all audiences into somewhat undifferentiated locals. Sakamoto himself was the backbone of the emerging repertory, joined by Darrell H. Y. Lum, one of the founders of *Bamboo Ridge*, while two major proponents of local Hawaiian plays gradually emerged in Victoria Nalani Kneubuhl and Alani Apio, and, most recently, the beginnings of a Hawaiian-language theatre in the work of Tammy Haili'ōpua Baker's company, Ka Hālau Hanakeaka. Complementing this has been the strong new strain of local prose fiction and poetry, which has interested mainland as well as resident readers and publishers and includes works by Lois-Ann Yamanaka, Nora Okja Keller, Darrell Lum, and Gary Pak. In the mid-1990s, Kumu Kahua had great success with readers' theatre adaptations of some of these works. The sum total of this artistic production has been a plurality, diversity, and moving beyond the manufacturing of predominantly positive or politically correct role models of the different groups for which social scientists (as distinct from many artists and spectators) have often wished.

It has always been difficult to define the demographics of local audiences and how their composition of ethnicities, age, personal and family histories, and so on are related to different varieties of local plays. Sakamoto's plays, however, have collectively been the biggest successes in box-office terms of all Kumu Kahua's offerings to date; and it also appears that especially Japanese American audiences have turned out in large numbers to support them. Sakamoto's favorite director, James Nakamoto, has stated that he thinks the plays have a special advance draw for middle-aged Asian Americans because of factors of nostalgia and the focus on immigrant family histories.[6]

It is even more difficult to generalize about reception on the mainland. Published reviews of mainland critics reveal a predictable pattern of comparison with mainstream American drama in which Sakamoto's work is found to have a slow tempo and a low "conflict" quotient but scores high on the grounds of character development and idiosyncratic and colorful dialogue. Few of these reviews exhibit much evidence of knowledge of the local context.[7]

However, one salient aspect to consider in respect to the demographics of mainland audiences is the sizeable expatriate community of Hawaiian islanders in Los Angeles and their patronage of the Los Angeles productions of Sakamoto's plays. According to F. Kathleen Foley in the *Los Angeles Times*, for example, the "specific references" in *Aloha Las Vegas*, in the Los Angeles season, brought "ripples of recognition from the Hawaiian expatriates" in the audience.[8] Director James Nakamoto estimated that over half of the audiences for the Japan America Theatre (Los Angeles) production of *Aloha Las Vegas* were Hawai'i expatriates; and Sakamoto himself thought that over two-thirds had Hawai'i backgrounds.[9] The smash-hit Los Angeles season of *Stew Rice* was partly due to expatriate audiences, some of whom came to see the production several times. It may be safely assumed that the percentage of Hawai'i expatriates in New York audiences for the Pan Asian Rep productions was considerably lower.[10]

Several mainland reviewers as well as local ones have noted the obsessive theme of displacement that recurs in Sakamoto's plays. Especially noteworthy are the remarks of Sylvie Drake, reviewing *Stew Rice* for the *Los Angeles Times* in its East West Players production: "These are young Hawaiians [*sic*] for whom moving to the Mainland is as big a deal as it would be for an Italian or an Irishman to immigrate to the

United States. . . . It is also about something the Italians and the Irish won't necessarily think about: whether to become 'haolified' or assimilated into the white culture."[11]

Central to Sakamoto's plays is the process of at least one character exploring what "home" means—how far it is indelibly connected to a physical locale of childhood and early maturity; and whether you carry home with you when you leave, how much of it you can take, how it changes you on relocation, and whether you can ever come "home" again. The nature and extent of personal sociocultural transformation in a new home is one common denominator of all Sakamoto's Hawai'i plays. This issue—presented, argued about, reiterated in various ways, from every direction, in all the plays—has no closure, no resolution.

Specifically, the dilemma is couched in terms of Hawai'i versus the mainland. Since the 1950s, the pendulum of the degree of attractiveness of the mainland has swung back and forth for Hawai'i long-time residents. At statehood, and into the early 1960s (as *Stew Rice, Mānoa Valley,* and *A'ala Park* attest), the mainland was for many an avenue to career advancement, personal freedom, and exposure to wider and more varied cultural traditions; but it was also a "place of pipedreams where driving can be of indefinite length and millionaire success comes easy."[12] In those years, the positive lures outweighed the negative; but by the 1970s, because of the health of Hawai'i's economy and the increasing plurality of cultural (mainstream and other) life-style options within the state, the pendulum swung the other way, many feeling happily content with lives and careers anchored firmly in the Islands. As a result of the economic uncertainties of recent years, many more are again leaving than arriving, and the expatriate Hawaiian populations of Los Angeles, Las Vegas, San Francisco, and other Western mainland cities are swelling.

"Mainland" is essentially a Janus-faced concept, with one face more prominent at some times than others: it is a place of greater freedom, broader cultural and professional horizons, and material opportunities —but also a place of greater competition, and of racial and ethnic discrimination where Asian Americans are a minority and face a potential loss of roots and local identity in the larger melting pot. This, then, is the ambiguity that all the plays investigate and to which all spectators of a Sakamoto play are invited to respond. Edward Sakamoto has lived out the local–mainland displacement dilemma himself; for over thirty years he has been a resident of Los Angeles, working much of the time as a copy editor at the *Los Angeles Times.* No wonder that the dilemma and the theme are so pervasive and deeply felt in all of the plays. Sakamoto has spoken eloquently in more than one interview of the irreconcilable pain of displacement, saying that he feels "in limbo" as an expatriate, and that "every time someone calls him an 'ex-Hawai'i' or 'former Hawai'i' resident, a little piece of him dies."[13] He has also said that he wants to come back to Hawai'i—but Hawai'i as it used to be, not as it is.[14] And of course much of this older Hawai'i is not only much changed but gone forever, like the neighborhood of A'ala Park in which Sakamoto grew up. As if positioning himself as the older Manny of *A'ala Park,* he has said: "You try to establish a certain kind of philosophy for why things happen the way they do. Sometimes, it's painful."[15]

❦

A'ala Park is the earliest and most revised of these three plays. It reflects, more than the others, an increasing complexity of tone and darkening of texture, especially as these relate to the relocation theme.

The genesis of the play can be traced back almost forty years to the one-act *In the Alley,* Sakamoto's first play, staged at the University of Hawai'i's Farrington Hall in 1961.[16] All of the major characters of that play reappear in *A'ala Park,* and the episode of the beating of the haole sailor, and the lead into it, are essentially the same. *A'ala Park* itself was written as one-half of a double bill for Los Angeles' East West Players presented in February 1980, titled *Hawai'i No Ka Oi*—the same title that Sakamoto later gave to his completed Kamiya trilogy. The other play on the bill was the first, shorter version of *Mānoa Valley,* so that in the original concept of the double bill, the umbrella title is ironic. Both plays are set in the year of statehood, but this event is seen from two very different perspectives—those of the middle-class "haves" of Mānoa Valley and the working-class "have-nots" of A'ala Park. In *Mānoa Valley,* Spencer Kamiya buoyantly prepares to leave for California, with his family's approval, to study aerospace engineering at USC. Manny, the hero of *A'ala Park,* leaves with no prospects except a temporary job at a gas station and delivers the parting shot: "I wish someday dey tear down dis whole area and cova 'um up wit' cement. I hate dis place. I hate dis island. I neva coming back to Hawaii."[17]

Although *A'ala Park* was the first half of the double bill, followed by the more optimistic (and better received) *Mānoa Valley,* the picture of local life given in the first play is the most uncompromisingly bitter ever penned by Sakamoto. At this point, there was no older Manny in the play to provide a more complex perspective. The play is more violent and brutal than its later incarnations. As in *In the Alley,* the beating of the haole sailor does not include the later justification for Manny's act of aggression—that the sailor is attempting to pick up Jeannie, Manny's girlfriend. In this earlier version, the sailor's female companion is a total stranger to the gang. In another scene of this first version, Manny rapes Jeannie at the climax of their argument rather than hitting her, as in the later versions.

In the next incarnation of the play, the first short full-length version staged by Kumu Kahua in 1984, there is some softening apparent. Here the "narrator," an older Manny, is introduced; but the device is still tentative and not entirely satisfactory, for Manny plays little part in the past and does not interact in any rich or complex way with his younger counterpart. Director Dando Kluever made the bonding of the gang rife with "macho" comic bravado and amusing physical attitudinizing as well as resentment, and the actor who played young Manny, Kevin Griffin, was both likeable and charismatic. Manny sported a picturesque period hat and an endearingly battered suitcase when leaving, so that the bitterness and severity of his final farewell to Hawai'i was mitigated and overlaid with a patina of nostalgia. Critics, while very positive about the evening, felt that the play had not quite reached its definitive form because the role and significance of the older Manny were elusive.[18]

The production was staged by Kumu Kahua under less than ideal circumstances at the old Hawaii Performing Arts Company theatre in Mānoa for a "dark night" series of Mondays and Tuesdays, against the inadequately disguised sets for Bolt's *A Man for All Seasons.* The box-office response prompted Kumu Kahua to investigate an extension at a larger space elsewhere, but actors' schedules prevented it. However, a revival of the play a mere two years later in a new production directed by Paul Cravath presented an opportunity for more people to experience the play at Leeward Community College near Pearl City in central Oʻahu in a 630-seat theatre with a full and picturesque setting on a proscenium stage.

Although the script underwent no further changes for Cravath's production, the less intimate presentation, along with the casting of the two Mannys, emphasized the bitterness of Manny's final rejection of Hawaiʻi. One critic felt that the deceptive nostalgia of the older Manny's opening narration was not really compatible with his bitterness at the end; the actor cast in this older role also suggested a character "much more polished and accomplished" than the younger character could plausibly have become. Again, the theatrical and thematic difficulties of the split-character device were remarked upon, and the "absence of closure" was criticized.[19]

The most recent version of the play was staged to acclaim at Kumu Kahua's Merchant Street theatre in the restored Kamehameha V Post Office building for a season beginning on May 1, 1997, directed by James A. Nakamoto. The downtown location of the theatre is only blocks from what remains of the old neighborhood of Aʻala Park. This version again sets off the two Mannys without providing a false consistency or wholeness in respect to the two; and it also evidences much more theatrical completion, and ingenuity as well, in the ways that the two Mannys interrelate throughout the play. This partly resulted from the casting of the actor Ray Bumatai as the older Manny. When Nakamoto sent Sakamoto audiotapes of Bumatai reading older Manny's monologues, Sakamoto was impressed and decided to expand the role.[20] Now, the Mannys took on a depth and complexity of interaction throughout. The intimate hundred-seat theatre, the deliberately claustrophobic skewed staging along the long end of the space, a threatening and decaying brick-scape designed by Alan Hunley, and the finely inflected work of an experienced cast created a sense that we were seeing the play in its fully realized form. Ray Bumatai and Warren Fabro brought out the counterpoint of the two manifestations of older and young Manny with aplomb—better than any other duo in earlier productions had done.

It is through this orchestration and articulation of the older and younger Mannys that Sakamoto also most effectively dramatizes his key theme of the choice between Hawaiʻi and the mainland and the passing into a kind of limbo of perpetual homelessness for characters who relocate. Older Manny begins the play "dressed in aloha shirt, trousers well-pressed," as if for commercial entertainment, and gives a ukulele-accompanied version of the 1940s standard "Manuela Boy." The reminiscences here are deceptively positive and nostalgic, and Aʻala Park in the period of the 1940s, small-kid time, are evoked. But then, as the action proper begins, the atmosphere darkens, and "there is quickly a troubled edge to the character" of the older Manny,[21] who in this version takes a much stronger part in reliving and participating in the remembered life, even as he is powerless to change it. In lines addressed to but unheard by his mother and Jeannie, older Manny says things that young Manny wanted to say at the time, or could have said but didn't. This older Manny stays aloof from the brutal beating of the haole sailor, but not from the knife-threatening and kicking of the mother's greasy, sponging lover. He remonstrates with his younger self, coaching and coaxing him to take actions he never took—most heartbreakingly, at the climax of the play. Older Manny is a scalpel to probe those complexities of human behavior and reaction that are beyond self-understanding, as well as the failures of communication between the characters that are not only young Manny's fault. Older Manny shares moments of introspection with his younger self; and, at one point he takes on the persona of his own father in a reminiscence of both the Mannys, when the father humiliated child Manny by calling him a "mother's boy" in front of a full bar at a hotel. In a happier vein, he shares ukulele playing and singing with young Manny. And he denies younger Manny's unequivocal "I neva coming back to Hawaii," protesting: " 'S wat you tink. You dunno wat you talking about. Go, you lolo asshole. See wat you get. No come cry in your damn beer later." But ultimately the bitter conclusion for the older Manny is that he will depart in his aloha shirt and slacks to do his musical gig for nostalgic visitors or expatriates, knowing all the time that the only way he will return to Hawaiʻi for good is "wen I ma-ke, die, dead. And not befo' dat. 'S why hard."

In respect to the play's major theme, the setting of the Aʻala Park location itself has special significance and poignancy (and it is also evoked at key moments of *Stew Rice,* and especially *Aloha Las Vegas.*) First, this was the area in which Sakamoto himself grew up. His family owned a store in the neighborhood, and some of the "small-kid time" reminiscences of playing in bomb shelters, and of crabs crawling up the side of culverts, are intensely personal. Now, unlike Mānoa Valley and many areas of the city evoked in *Stew Rice* and *Aloha Las Vegas*, Aʻala Park as a distinctive neighborhood is gone for good. In the 1950s, it was still a complex, low-income neighborhood of wood-framed buildings and "narrow, dusty alleys,"[22] close enough to both the docking tourist cruise boats on the waterfront and to River Street, where the brothel business peaked during World War II. The nucleus of the neighborhood was the actual Aʻala Park and its bandstand, famous for political meetings and outdoor concerts, and also containing several bars and theatres that showed Japanese, Chinese, and Filipino movies. Aʻala Park, then, was a raffish, violent, but picturesque neighborhood—all razed shortly after statehood and now replaced by a characterless and artificial rolling expanse of "grass, shade trees, homeless people, and the occasional scavenger."[23]

Second, Aʻala Park was a true working-class neighborhood, and indeed, this version of *Aʻala Park* is the grimmest and most working-class-oriented of all Sakamoto's plays to date. For those who go to the mainland from here, the choices may well be no more liberating than they were at home, and just as desperate. As Uji, the old pool-hall proprietor, says to Manny: "I work on one freighta and sail to the mainland. Was junk ova dere. Dose days was hard fo' guys like us. If you not white, you hard luck. . . . But I still think Hawaii betta fo' people like us. We all stick togedda, no pilikia. Up dere, you going be all alone." As Manny's closing narration makes clear, some of the others' escapes from the neighborhood were only ostensible escapes: Champ went to Maui, but to farm the onions he hated; Cabral to the military, only to die in Vietnam; Bear to cab driving; and Jojo to Castle & Cook. So the dominating metaphor of *Aʻala Park* seems to be that of the tiny ant surrounded by a ring of spit, unable to crawl out, and, in the end, returning to the imprisonment of a small crack in the cement.

❦

Stew Rice had a much shorter gestation period than *Aʻala Park*, but a similar darkening and deepening of the play's tone and character development are apparent from one version to another (and, of course, within the play itself, for the act 1 scenes of nostalgic comic goofiness are held up to ironic examination in the much more downbeat developments of act 2). Sakamoto wrote the play especially for Kumu Kahua. The premiere of the first version opened in a production at Kawaiahao Theatre, Mid-Pacific Institute, a private school in Mānoa, on May 7, 1987, and toured the neighboring islands of Kauaʻi, Maui, and Hawaiʻi during June. This was the last Kumu Kahua production to open at the Mid-Pacific space, which had hosted Kumu Kahua for the previous four years. The company was given notice to make way for a rival theatre company, which had offered to run acting and technical theatre classes for MPI students. Kumu Kahua faced daunting difficulties in finding makeshift theatrical spaces for the following season, and in addition there were problems with rehearsal space. These pressures were compounded by casting problems for the female roles of *Stew Rice*. It was not too surprising that Dando Kluever's production was somewhat distracted and out-of-focus; critics were disappointed, and the play was the first local play of Sakamoto's to garner just an adequate box-office response in Hawaiʻi. Critics complained about lack of definition and attractiveness of the characters, and a mere rehashing on the playwright's part of old thematic concerns without making positive statements about them.[24]

Sakamoto revised the play for a production at Los Angeles' East West Players that opened in January 1988. Main revisions consisted of additional emphasis on pop songs to define mood and to set the period in various scenes, and reduction of the cast to six characters by excising a speech-teacher role. Dana Lee directed this production, which was warmly received by Los Angeles critics and so popular that it had a return season. It won Sakamoto a Hollywood Drama-Logue award.

These alterations, especially the elimination of a character, were substantial, and further significant changes were made to the play for its Kumu Kahua revival in September 1995, at the group's Kamehameha V Post Office theatre. The production was directed by James Nakamoto, who was surprised to see that Jason Scott Lee was present at the auditions. Lee, whose popularity was then at its zenith after his starring roles in three Hollywood feature movies, was keen to do stage work in an intimate setting while home between film projects. He was cast, somewhat against type, as homebody Zippy. When Sakamoto heard of the casting, he set to work to make the Zippy character less mellow and laid-back. He considerably revised Zippy's climactic final speech: this now became a stinging rejection of his two relocated friends—more of which below.[25] The participation of Jason Scott Lee no doubt helped to secure full houses for the entire run before the play even opened. Several more performances and two extensions were added.

James Nakamoto, in his program note, stated that in his production he wished to stress the theme of male friendship—its definition and limitations. However, the script itself, even in the opening character notes on the "Cast" page, makes it clear that Sakamoto once again had at the forefront the theme of relocation from Hawai'i and its consequences. It is clear that the rupture of friendships among the central male trio here is symbiotically tied in with this issue, and that it dominates the characterization of Russell, Ben, and Zippy. The three women in the play are meant to be peripheral, though they too at various times discuss the merits and disadvantages of "going mainland."

Before looking at the characterization, it should be noted that, in this play but not the other two, the dichotomy between pidgin and standard English is important in defining and refining aspects of Sakamoto's major theme. The dialogue here provides a reliable and dexterous calibration of the characters' attitudes, at different points of their lives, to the mainland–local dichotomy. Russell, a high school junior inspired by his teacher to speak standard English well, nevertheless slips back into pidgin with his buddies in act 2. Ben, who speaks pidgin even in his high school valedictorian speech in act 1, barely uses pidgin at all, with anyone, in act 2. And Zippy, who uses pidgin exclusively, reverts to standard English only in his final denunciation of Ben and Russell. Standard English, as a symbol both of assimilation for mainland expatriates and of the cultural colonization of Hawai'i, was an issue of even greater focus in the first version of the play, where the character of the teacher, then called "Miss Fletcher," appeared in several scenes of language coaching. In act 2, there was also an interesting scene in which Russell visits her at his old school. He has an old crush on her, which is one reason for the visit, but he also wants to thank her for enabling him to realize the importance of "what I had to know . . . and tell you how important your speech classes were to me."[26]

As for the characters in *Stew Rice,* the equivalent of Manny in *A'ala*

Park is Russell Shima, here more clearly the authorial surrogate in that Russell is a journalist, a movie critic with a Los Angeles paper. He appears as both narrator and character in the major action. This time the narration is less important than in the earlier play and is used purely as a framing device: it does not interweave with nor provide any contrapuntal distancing device from the scenes set in 1957 and 1978. Nevertheless, in his narrations Russell is not simply exuding positive nostalgia —far from it. The narration is disconcertingly revealed as largely ironic, and it contains several subtle self-lacerations. Russell tells the audience: "To be frank, the twenty years are a blur to me. I was very insular. . . . I didn't pay enough attention to the historical events unfolding around me" (act 2). In the action itself, Russell is the *raisonneur* of the three, the most perceptive, the most articulate, the most self-deprecating, and the least impulsive and passionate. He has never married. His reunion with Donna is a well-intentioned miss. His career as movie critic, though he protests too much that it makes him happy, is also a kind of escape from engagement with reality: "I found real life boring so I sought out dark sanctums of fantasy" (act 2). Moreover, his pronouncements on various movies and movie stars inspire little confidence about his critical acuity, and he apparently needs to eke out his slender salary as a reviewer by writing coffee-table books on past Hollywood glitterati and movie star folklore. But, in the climactic scene of accounting with Ben and Zippy, when the crab nets come in empty, he states the mainland–local theme more explicitly and clearly than any other Sakamoto character, when he says to Ben:

> We don't belong in Hawaii anymore. We're displaced persons. Out in limbo. Neither here nor there. Sure, we try to fit in, we make believe like we're haoles, but the haoles will always look at us like we're foreigners, aliens with funny eyes and yellow skin living in their white society. Maybe what we were searching for was in Hawaii all along. (act 2)

Russell is also the temporizer and peacemaker as the rift widens between the other two buddies, Ben and Zippy.

Certainly Ben is the most extroverted, impulsive, and insensitive of the three. The foundation for his later development is securely laid in act

1, but in act 2 we have a fully fledged portrait of the "mature" Ben. His confidences to Ruby about why, after a tour of duty in Vietnam, he quit his calling as a doctor to become a stock-market analyst are glibly phrased and uninvolved, almost as if he were talking about himself in the third person. His argument, essentially, is that he liked a good income but didn't want to make it in a medical system that discriminates between rich and poor. Ruby is not convinced. "Very idealistic, aren't you?" she says with knowing irony, and a little later, "What makes you happy, that's the important thing" (act 2). It is Ben who is most estranged from Hawai'i. He can't remember the names of the suburbs his Waikiki hotel looks out on any more, can't live in his old family home because of arguments with his parents over his life and career choices, and is openly critical of Hawai'i to Zippy. His paean to the attractions of New York City sounds like a TV commercial, and he directly patronizes Zippy by opining that "if you had gone to the mainland . . . [it] would have been good for you. Broaden your horizons, that sort of thing" (act 2). He says that in New York he exclusively dates younger haole women—after an unsuccessful marriage to a haole wife. Most crucially, at the climax, Ben tactlessly reveals to Shima in Zippy's presence the real reason that Zippy did not go to the mainland in 1958 and discloses, finally, that for him assimilation with the haoles on the mainland has been the price he had to pay for learning to survive cutthroat style and beat down the competition, dealing the cards with "my back to the wall" (act 2).

However, it is the character of Zippy that forms the main conduit for the play's darkening of tone, both during the transition from act 1 to act 2, and also in its developmental process from first to final version. Zippy seems the sunniest and most laid-back of the three main characters. In Act 1, he is the one who is most vulnerable and naive—he can't even dance, and envies Russell and Ben's greater articulateness and confidence. In act 2, though a proud father of two and happily married to Sharon, he is clearly slipping into sexual and social routines, and tells about an instance when his social services personnel manager job so exhausted him that he fell asleep in the bathtub. He increasingly chafes under the overt criticism and patronization of Ben. When his plan to re-create a favorite memory of their youth, the crabbing bonanza, fails miserably, and Ben reveals the reason why Zippy didn't join them in going to the mainland, his resentment of his former friends comes out; he delivers a final devastating diatribe against the other two and exits for good. This speech was much milder in the earlier version of the play. In its final version, it is excoriating:

> Look, no feel sorry for me. 'Cause you da one gotta feel sorry. And I'm gonna tell you this in good English, so you understand. I'm glad now that I didn't go to the mainland, not if I had to turn out like you. I got a good family, lots of friends and relatives around me. I got a good life, I got more than you'll ever have. Go back to the mainland, with all your haole girlfriends and your haole lifestyle. Who cares about that kind of life? Who wants it? Big deal, big shot. Do Hawaii a favor—don't come back. We don't need you. (act 2)

In the first production of *Stew Rice,* Keith Kashiwada portrayed Zippy as an even-tempered, ever sociable character, at the end disappointed in his friends and sad rather than angry, and this was supported by the earlier script. In the 1995 Kumu Kahua revival, Jason Scott Lee's Zippy from the start was clearly a more restless and passionate individual, and Sakamoto not only rewrote his final speech but made several other smaller adjustments to the role in earlier scenes.[27] Zippy's final denunciation thus became the charged highlight of the production, hanging in the air over the final moments of Russell's closing narration.

Ultimately the play charts the failure of friendship between these men who have made different choices about Hawai'i or the mainland. All of them are dissatisfied: "None of their motives have been pure. None of their compromises have been satisfying. None of their facades are unblemished."[28] In Russell's valedictory narration, it was the line "you always see something new in your life every time you play it back" which located, in critic Joseph T. Rozmiarek's opinion, "the best definition of searching for lost feeling" in the work[29]—a search that also preoccupies Manny in *A'ala Park.*

So, once again, there is a lack of closure in the play; and, once again, the sum total of *Stew Rice* is not a simple, life-affirming positive empathy with either the characters or the situation, but something much more equivocal and problematic. The key metaphor, perhaps not quite as desperate as the spit-covered ant in the crack of *A'ala Park,* is a wholesome bowl of stew rice with a cockroach in it.

❦

Aloha Las Vegas, the most recent of the plays published here, evolved from an unfortunate and then fortuitous series of personal experiences of the playwright. He had considered writing a play set in Las Vegas, a city he had visited and enjoyed, in which a group of unrelated people go from Honolulu on a "junket" tour, but this premise proved intractable. Sakamoto was also having difficulties with an early version of *The Taste of Kona Coffee,* and illness in 1989 was a further setback. Visiting Honolulu for the Kumu Kahua production of his mainland-set play *Pilgrimage* in 1991, the playwright was delighted by the work of the cast and the director James Nakamoto and felt suddenly reenergized; a subsequent visit to Las Vegas, where some relatives had moved, produced a breakthrough realization that the Vegas play would have to involve a whole family, who would relocate there from Hawai'i. It was also brought home to Sakamoto how many expatriates were already living in Las Vegas, or were moving there.[30] This included a sizeable exodus of property-rich, cash-poor families who had sold and moved during the real-estate boom of the late 1980s—a bubble of inflated values that was to burst in the early 1990s. Between 1987 and 1990, the median asking price of a home nearly doubled, from $185,000 to $352,000.[31] Since that time, though prices of property have stabilized at a lower level, the exodus of many local residents has continued for other reasons —principally, the recession that began in 1994 and deepened with the collapse of the Asian tourist market in late 1997. So, although *Aloha Las Vegas* was very topical in Hawai'i at the time it was written, it is still so today, as the Hawaiian job market continues to be depressed and Las Vegas continues to thrive.

So far the play has had just two productions: James Nakamoto's for Kumu Kahua Theatre, which opened in September 1992 in the newly renovated Tenney Theatre, a production that was then remounted with only one cast change to play in Los Angeles in the downtown Japan America Theatre for a limited season in June 1994; and Ron Nakahara's staging for the Pan Asian Rep in New York in April 1998. The Nakamoto production, in the not very intimate venue of Tenney, with its awkwardly high and narrow stage and assertive proscenium, stressed the comic aspects of the play; these, and the necessarily punchy delivery, enhanced all the positive ramifications of Wally's decision to relocate. The production was the biggest box-office success of any Kumu Kahua production up to that time: the three hundred-seat theatre was sold out for several nights and the run had to be extended for several additional performances. In spite of this success, some of us felt that the ambivalent complexity of Wally's reasons for his decision, and its darker implications as revealed in act 2, scenes 2 and 3, did not entirely register. This was also because of two standout performances of supporting actors in primarily comic roles—Nan Asuncion as Gracie, and Dann Seki as Alvin. Nakahara's New York production, in a more intimate venue, was nevertheless by report no less comic than the Honolulu production, and was especially notable for Kati Kuroda's performance as Gracie.[32]

This emphasis on comedy did not entirely obscure the point that, along with *The Life of the Land, Aloha Las Vegas* is the most Chekhovian of all Sakamoto's plays, as was noted by both local and mainland reviewers. Here, Sakamoto eschews the "privileged narrator" technique; therefore it is not a memory play in the sense that "times gone by" are re-created through a character's "looking back." However, the soul of the play lies in the reminiscences of several characters, so that the past is poignantly alive in the present throughout the play. The heart of the play is act 2, scene 2, when Wally and his daughter, June, recall Wally's dead wife, Kay, and their son, Butch, sleepily crosses the stage to comment that "da room still get da same smell. Mama smell." This scene evokes the sleepy, homecoming tone of act 1 of *The Cherry Orchard,* and the final leave-taking of act 2, scene 3 even more clearly conjures up the final act of Chekhov's play. But it is the way in which character shapes action, and is more significant than action, that most stamps the play as Chekhovian, as two reviewers remarked.[33] Not a great deal happens, and what does happen is fairly predictable. Nevertheless, ". . . for a couple of hours, the characters come and go in the living room of a Honolulu bungalow, doing little but talking, and you care about every one of them down to the last line."[34]

Once again, the "local versus mainland" theme is central here; and Sakamoto has never presented it with more poignancy. Much of the comedy of the play—including the arresting opening riff where Gracie "wins" $64,000 at craps—has a thematic if not linear purpose: to make palpable the lunatic contagion of Las Vegas and the aura it exudes.

Though the text of the final scene makes it appear that Wally, a sixty-five-year-old retired baker, does not regret his decision to relocate, the subtext of this same scene, and the subtleties of the characterization of the Vegas spokesman, Harry, suggest a different implication.

Harry is an interesting character, likeable enough but also a sleazy manipulator—not a character with whom a local or any other spectator would easily identify. We learn a considerable amount about him, almost none of it good. He is now a professional gambler in Vegas, and survives by "control," cannily playing the slots. "Control" is a philosophy of moderation when on a winning streak and knowing when to stop, but it is a concept that he himself mostly defines, and so it becomes increasingly suspect when evoked by the others—especially Wally and Butch. Even first impressions of Harry are not favorable. "How do I look?" he asks Wally on his first entrance (act 1, scene 1), significantly not complimenting Wally on how *he* looks. Revealed as selfish and sexist—both qualities that had apparently contributed to his failed marriage—he boasts of having Wayne Newton as a "buddy" and "guarantees" jobs in real estate and security for Butch and his wife; and he extols the virtues of the California Hotel, center of the local Hawaiian community in Vegas. In Honolulu he puts on the dog by staying at the upscale Halekulani Hotel, famous for its old-world charm and cachet of class. Later we learn that he flunked out of Central Intermediate school and that it was only Wally's interest in him as a slightly older mentor figure that straightened him out. He skilfully plays throughout on tinsel visions of Las Vegas as a paradise, especially for retirees who can feel when they play the slots and win that "Dey did 'um all by demselves" (act 1, scene 1). Harry's plan for him and Wally to make their living—opening an island-style shave-ice concession on the strip, with ice cream or azuki beans in the bottom—is a scheme that could conceivably click with haoles as well as locals. His Disneyfied paeans to the city, as June remarks, makes it sound like he might be employed by the Las Vegas Chamber of Commerce.

But his vision includes one factor that the Manny of *A'ala Park* and the buddies of *Stew Rice* did not have as reassurance—that Wally will not be alone on the mainland. As a retiree, he will be part of the expatriate community centered around the California Hotel, sharing the collective experiences of euphoria and joy that Harry so repeatedly extols.

Still, the most potent part of Harry's argument, and the most persuasive because it evokes Wally's own sense of guilt and alienation, is the nostalgia Harry evokes to suggest that the old Hawai'i is gone forever —and a central image here is the old A'ala Park:

> W'en I was young, Aala Park was one lively place . . . real festive atmosphere. Today Aala Park look so small, so diff'rent. Get da sign Aala Street, but no mo' street. All covered up wit' grass. Aala Street use to have tenement houses and lodda stores making business. Today nuttin'. . . . No mo' life. You see, Wally, 's why you betta come to Vegas. Not our Hawaii anymore. (act 2, scene 1)

For Wally, the old, vanished A'ala Park is the site of his cherished first meeting with his wife in a saimin stand where she was a waitress, a memory he shares with June in act 2, scene 2. The old home he lives in reminds him continually of her—and of his own guilt for her death, because it was the secondary smoke from his smoking habit which was responsible for the cancer that killed her. The poignancy of this confession, and the play's shaping of guilt and a degree of absolution to move beyond it, is clinched by a more recent, positive memory: Kay's delight at winning at the slots in Vegas six months before she died. All this triggers a decision to move that June knows, and Wally also knows, may well prove to be the wrong one.

Like the corresponding scene in *The Cherry Orchard,* the brief final scene evokes the counterpointing motifs of saying goodbye to the old local life and looking forward to a new one. June, for so long the rational reason why Wally has been reluctant to leave, is provided for by her engagement to Alvin, and is pregnant as well. She has clearly and positively grown out of the delimiting father-daughter bond of her previous experience. This is comically and touchingly underlined by the last family portrait taken in the old home, in which she, for the last time, agrees to sit on her father's lap. Although Wally seems upbeat about the move, the positivism is constantly called into question.

This ambivalence constitutes a held tension, as some crucial doubts about the move remain unresolved. The son, Butch, is clearly in danger of not being able to "control" his gambling in Vegas—something already hinted at by his past history there. Moreover, his wife, Dee-Dee, has allowed him to believe that he might still be able to become a father in Vegas—a pipe dream, as her confidence to June has earlier revealed. Wally knows he'll miss Gracie, the Firs-like servant figure left alone in the house at the end, playing the Sinatra number "Time After Time," Wally's way of evoking his memories and old life with Kay, as she forlornly contemplates Wally's gift of the last guava chiffon cake that he will ever make. Throughout, the place-names of Hawai'i, the icons of defunct sports heroes and customs and place-names, are not included in the play merely for nostalgic recognition and local identification but as indexes of a special place, time, and culture that Wally is about to renounce. June is much more doggedly loyal. As she argues in act 2, scene 2: "I'm staying because Hawaii is our home. We belong here, not on da Mainland. The Fukuda family has been in Hawaii a hundred years." To which Wally replies, "Butch can bring my ashes back, so we going be here foreva and eva." This is not so far removed, after all, from the final lines of older Manny in *A'ala Park.*

The central metaphor of this play—in contrast to the ant of *A'ala Park* and the stew with cockroach of *Stew Rice*—is the jigsaw puzzle on the coffee table, which Wally wrestles with but never completes.

Thus, we see that all Sakamoto's protagonists in these plays are ultimately displaced, questioning their own decisions made, some wondering whether renegotiation of those decisions is possible. And this brings us full circle to why the responsive spectator—Asian American or otherwise, local or otherwise—finds it difficult to respond unproblematically to these plays and to empathize with these protagonists. For the actions, choices, and decisions of Manny, Ben, Russell, Zippy, and Wally are always so presented that positive affirmations are held in abeyance. Closure is never really achieved; cultural identity is problematic; home is elusive. Behind the reassuring laughter at the recognizable—the box-office-boosting carapace of any local Sakamoto play—the troubling theme of the enigma of displacement remains.

NOTES

1. This has been noted by several earlier commentators and reviewers. Bert Narimasu, then an M.A. student at the UHM Theatre and Dance Department, wrote a perceptive unpublished essay on this aspect of Sakamoto's work in the 1980s; most recently, Franklin Odo mentioned it in his Introduction to *Hawai'i No Ka Oi: The Kamiya Family Trilogy* (Honolulu: University of Hawai'i Press, 1995), xviii–xix.

2. Josephine Lee, *Performing Asian America: Race and Ethnicity on the Contemporary Stage* (Philadelphia: Temple University Press, 1997), 28.

3. Audience reception theory has developed recently into an influential and valuable way to image the kind of audience reaction and response that may exist beyond published and citable reviews of plays. It takes into consideration factors such as the social and environmental context and audience demographics. See especially Susan Bennett, *Theatre Audiences: A Theory of Production and Reception,* 2d ed. (London and New York: Routledge, 1997); and Alan Read, *Theatre and Everyday Life: An Ethics of Performance* (London and New York: Routledge, 1993).

4. Frankin Odo, in his Foreword to Sakamoto's *Hawai'i No Ka Oi: The Kamiya Family Trilogy* (Honolulu: University of Hawai'i Press, 1995), dealt with some of the pertinent factors, especially as they relate to local Asian Americans. Though an Asian American–dominated Democratic Party has been in power since 1954, the confidence of local Asian American hegemony has been eroding since at least the 1970s, with the influx of new immigrant groups such as the Vietnamese and the Samoans, and shifting population demographics that have superseded the Japanese American majority of earlier times (xiv–xix.)

5. Jonathan Y. Okamura, "Why There Are No Asian Americans in Hawai'i: The Continuing Significance of Local Identity," *Social Process in Hawai'i* 35 (1994): 161.

6. James A. Nakamoto, interview by author, tape recording, Kumu Kahua Theatre, Honolulu, April 19, 1999.

7. See, for example, J. Kathleen Foley's review *"Aloha Las Vegas* Stays on Hawai'i Time," *Los Angeles Times,* June 20, 1994, sec. F, p. 7; Julius Novick, "Paradise Island," a review of *The Life of the Land,* performed by Pan Asian Repertory, New York, *Village Voice,* June 23, 1987, 98; and Mel Gussow, "Stage: Edward Sakamoto's *Mānoa Valley,*" a review of *Mānoa Valley,* also performed by Pan Asian Repertory, *New York Times,* Feb. 25, 1985, 11.

8. Foley, *"Aloha Las Vegas* Stays on Hawai'i Time."

9. Nakamoto interview; Edward Sakamoto, telephone conversation with author, April 20, 1999.

10. Both Sakamoto and Nakamoto concurred on this.

11. Sylvie Drake, "*Stew Rice:* Nostalgia and Reality," *Los Angeles Times,* Jan. 11, 1988, sec. VI, p. 5.

12. John W. White, "Revival of *A'ala Park* Funny But Too Focused," *Honolulu Star-Bulletin,* Nov. 3, 1986, sec. C, p. 3.

13. Mike Gordon, "Haunted By Ghosts of His Past," *Honolulu Star-Bulletin,* May 5, 1988, sec. B, p. 6.

14. Wayne Muromoto, "Aloha, Ed Sakamoto," *Hawaii Herald,* Oct. 2, 1992, sec. A, p. 16.

15. Gordon, "Haunted By Ghosts of His Past," sec. B, p. 1.

16. The play was published in *Kumu Kahua Plays,* ed. Dennis Carroll (Honolulu: University of Hawai'i Press, 1983), 123–142.

17. *A'ala Park,* first version, courtesy of Sakamoto, t.s. [1981], unpaginated.

18. Pierre Bowman, in his review in the *Honolulu Star-Bulletin,* stated that "the play does not give the audience a complete picture. . . . The older Manny is longing for his past, but what the audience sees gives little hint about the things that shape this nostalgia" ("A Vivid Slice of Life from Hawaii of Old," March 21, 1984, sec. B, p. 4.); and Joseph T. Rozmiarek, in the *Honolulu Advertiser,* remarked, "We need to see the tragedy of the older Manny and to have drawn for us the link between the two natures" ("Sakamoto's *Aala Park:* A Gem," March 21, 1984, sec. C, p. 8).

19. Rozmiarek, "New *A'ala* Takes on Bitter Tone," *Honolulu Advertiser,* Nov. 3, 1986, sec. B, p. 3.

20. Sakamoto, telephone conversation with author.

21. Rozmiarek, "*A'ala Park* Is a Rich, Nostalgic Reflection on Life," *Honolulu Advertiser,* May 5, 1997, sec. C, p. 4.

22. Burl Burlingame, "A'ala Revisited," *Honolulu Star-Bulletin,* May 1, 1997, sec. B, p. 1.

23. Ibid.

24. See Joseph T. Rozmiarek, "*Stew Rice* Goes Home Again—With Problems," *Honolulu Advertiser,* May 9, 1987, sec. D, pp. 2–3; John W. White, "*Stew Rice* is a Tasty Recipe, But Needs a Little More Meat," *Honolulu Star-Bulletin,* May 8, 1987, sec. B, p. 2.

25. Nakamoto interview and Sakamoto telephone conversation with author.

26. *Stew Rice,* First Version, courtesy of Mr. Sakamoto, unpaginated t.s. [1986], act 2.

27. Nakamoto interview and Sakamoto conversation.

28. Joseph T. Rozmiarek, "*Stew Rice:* A Slice of Local Life," *Honolulu Advertiser,* Sept. 8, 1995, sec. C, p. 3.

29. Ibid.

30. Sakamoto telephone conversation.

31. Will Hoover, "In the Hole," *Sunday Star-Bulletin and Advertiser,* Feb. 21, 1999, sec. E, p. 1.

32. J. D. R. Bruckner, in his review "Where Hawaiians Discover Paradise," *New York Times,* April 23, 1998, sec. E, p. 5, singles out Kuroda for special praise.

33. Ibid.; Rozmiarek, "The Local Appeal of Las Vegas," *Honolulu Advertiser,* Sept. 22, 1992, sec. B, p. 3.

34. Bruckner, "Where Hawaiians Discover Paradise."

A'ala Park

Cast of Characters

OLDER MANNY, age forty-five to fifty-five

MANNY, about twenty, with dark, brooding eyes

JOJO, Manny's brother, about fourteen

MAMA, their mother, about forty-five

BEAR, Manny's buddy, burly, mean-looking but good-natured

JEANIE, Manny's girlfriend

CHAMP, built like boxer, age nineteen

CABRAL, a lanky Portuguese, age nineteen

SLICK, Mama's boyfriend, a greasy type in his late thirties

UJI, local Japanese man, late sixties

SWEENEY, a white sailor in his mid-twenties

TIME: Late summer 1959, the year of statehood

PLACE: A low-income section of Honolulu, in A'ala Park area

SCENERY: The main playing area is an alley with a wall of gangrenous-green, peeling paint and termite-ridden wood. There is a beat-up trash can. At stage left is a back door which leads to an unseen pool hall. At stage right on an elevated platform are a table and two chairs, a section of Manny's tenement home.

Act One

(*The stage is dark. A ukulele is being strummed. Slowly a soft spotlight expands upstage.* OLDER MANNY, *dressed in an aloha shirt, trousers, and shoes, enters. He is playing the uke and singing "Manuela Boy." When he finishes, he addresses the audience.*)

OLDER MANNY: Aeh, you like dat song? Old, yeah. Bet you neva hear 'um long time. Someting li'dat pop in your head, and you wonda, chee, where dat wen' come from? I used to live A'ala Park side. No kidding. Dat whole area, you know—King Street, Beretania, Hotel Street, River Street. You know where da river flow into da ocean, I used to t'row stones from da wall at da small crabs crawling up da side. You too? Okay, anodda street was Liliha, Vineyard Street still dere, yeah? But Hall Street gone, right? Rememba da theaters around dere. Park Theatre, Honolulu Theatre, International Theatre, Toyo Theatre. All dere by Aʻala Park. Da real park, I mean. Chee, I can rememba wen da park had bomb sheltas. Yeah, in da forties, wartime. Grassy mounds all ova da park. I used to get cardboard boxes and slide down da bomb sheltas. Good fun. But inside was spooky—for one kid. Dark, cobwebs, dirt. Any minute you tink one ghost going come out. Aeh, and I always used to enjoy watching da Filipino guys in one circle kicking da small bamboo ball in one game called sipa-sipa. Yeah, 's how far back I go. But all dat was small kid time. Now I like take you back to 1959, da year of statehood, when I was olda. In dose days da place I used to live was someting like dis.

(*Lights up slowly on the set.*)

Brings back memories, man. Lotsa memories.

(*UJI, the proprietor of the pool hall, enters through the back door, wearing white undershirt, baggy pants, and rubber slippers. He busily sweeps the area with a broom.*)

'S old man Uji. He run da pool hall and cook little bit on da side.

(*UJI sweeps and hums an old Japanese song. Now he stops and sniffs what is clearly a foul odor coming from the trash can. He pokes into the can with the broom handle, sniffing. BEAR enters from the opposite end of the stage, wearing a soiled T-shirt, blue jeans, and rubber slippers. He watches UJI from a distance.*)

'S my buddy, Bear. Ugly bugga, eh.

(*UJI dips his head into the can and jerks it back up. Yeah, it smells bad in there. BEAR saunters over and taps UJI on the shoulder. The startled UJI drops his broom and spins around.*)

BEAR: Wat you doing, Uji?

UJI: Aeh, next time you make noise wen you walk. You like give me one heart attack? If I wen' die, I come back like one obake and get you.

(*UJI raises his arms high and strikes a ghostlike pose, staring at BEAR with a grotesque expression.*)

BEAR: Aeh, aeh, aeh, no make li'dat. You look spooky, man. . . . Wat you get?

(*OLDER MANNY sits and watches the action. BEAR peers into the can and smells the odor.*)

BEAR: One dead cat. Stink like-a hell.

UJI: Who put 'um dere?

BEAR: No look at me. Dis where us guys hang out, we not going make 'um smelly.

UJI: Help me, help me.

BEAR: Wat?

UJI: T'row in da riva.

BEAR: Dat no good. Mo' betta t'row 'um in da alley next to da fish market. Ova dere stink all da time anyway.

UJI: Okay, you take 'um.

(UJI hands him the bag containing the cat.)

BEAR: No, you take.

UJI: No, you take.

BEAR: I no touch nuttin' dead.

UJI: Wassamadda you, you big boy!

BEAR: Yeah, 'cause I no mess wit' da kahuna.

UJI: You go and I make saimin fo' you.

BEAR: Aeh, no fair, you talking to my stomach.

UJI: Yeah, I make you opu happy.

(UJI pats BEAR's stomach as he hands him the bag. BEAR takes it at arm's length and starts to exit.)

BEAR: Make da saimin ono, eh.

UJI: No worry, I put extra plenny char siu fo' you.

BEAR: Chee, t'anks, eh, Uji, you all right.

(BEAR exits. UJI resumes sweeping. He has his back to CHAMP, who appears, shadow-boxing silently. He's wearing a sweatshirt without sleeves and swimming shorts, and is bare-foot. CHAMP is behind UJI now.)

CHAMP: Aeh, Uji!

(UJI is startled again.)

I wen' scare you?

UJI: Wassamadda wit' everybody. Me one old man, you know, no good give me heart attack.

CHAMP: Sorry, eh. Us boxers gotta be light on our feet. Aeh, but no worry, us guys take care of you.

(CHAMP shadow-boxes again; he's not too swift with hands and feet.)

UJI: You get one boxing match coming up?

CHAMP: Yeah, gotta keep in shape. Tarrific, eh?

UJI: No get hurt dis time. I see you get beat up, make my body sore.

CHAMP: Aeh, how you tink I feel?

UJI: Bam, bam, bam, down, eight, nine, ten. Pau. Da end.

CHAMP: I neva look dat bad, eh?

(JEANIE enters in red shorts and a yellow sleeveless blouse. She also wears rubber slippers.)

JEANIE: Hi, Uji, Champ. You folks see Manny around?

UJI: Not today.

CHAMP: Try check da bandstand. I tink he practicing wit' his uke.

JEANIE: Yeah, t'anks.

(She exits.)

OLDER MANNY: 'S my girl, Jeanie. Cute, eh?

(CABRAL enters, pedaling a homemade scooter, made with a two-by-four and roller-skate wheels.)

CABRAL: Aeh, Champ, hurry up. Time fo' roadwork.

CHAMP: Let da road rest. You no can see I busy talking?

CABRAL: Sorry, eh, Uji. But I gotta get dis slacka ready fo' da fight. Not going be easy. He need all da help he can get. He fool around too much.

CHAMP: No listen to him. One week befo' da fights, I no fool around wit' da wahines.

CABRAL: Big deal. C'mon, get dose legs in shape.

CHAMP: Look, Cabral, you no watch out I get dese legs in shape on your head.

CABRAL: Yeah? I like see. C'mon, try catch me.

(CABRAL pedals slowly away, baiting CHAMP.)

CHAMP: See you, Uji. I gotta teach dis Portogee one good lesson.

(CABRAL exits laughing, with CHAMP right behind him. BEAR enters from the opposite direction.)

BEAR: Aeh, Champ, wait. Aeh, you buggas!

UJI: Wat happen to da cat?

BEAR: I put 'um where he going be happy—right dere wit' da dead fishes.

UJI: No make trouble, eh.

BEAR: No trouble. You neva make my saimin yet? You said you going put extra char siu inside, eh, how come I rate?

UJI: We go inside. I going open up da pool hall.

BEAR: I help you rack up da balls. Rememba, eh, anybody give you bad time, you just tell me. I fix him up good. And you gotta watch who you pay off on da pinballs. No can trust some guys, dey pilau.

(*They exit through the back door.*)

OLDER MANNY: Man, dose guys look so young. If only we can stay li'dat and not get old. But if you no grow old, den you no can learn too. 'S right, eh. You stay young, you stay stupid. You no learn from your mistakes. But den maybe you learn everyting too late and den wat. Wait. Now you going see one good-looking guy come in wit' Jeanie. 'S going be me wen I was young. No be surprised if da body dif- f'rent. Afta all, was, wat, long, long time ago.

(*MANNY and JEANIE enter and go past OLDER MANNY. He's wearing a faded maroon basketball jersey and jeans. He's barefoot and strums a ukulele.*)

JEANIE: You serious about going to da Mainland?

MANNY: Yeah. I figga someday I going up.

JEANIE: Why you like leave Hawai'i for?

MANNY: Wat get here? Nuttin'. Dis place just like one prison, living on one rock, so damn small, no can breathe. Shit, take you just half a day drive around da island.

JEANIE: So wat? Who tell you drive so fast? If you go slow take one whole day.

MANNY: Sometimes I like just drive and drive, just me and nobody else, and I keep on driving till nobody around but me. And den I yell my head off till I go deaf and lose my voice da same time.

JEANIE: Wat good dat going do?

(*OLDER MANNY joins the two.*)

MANNY: Going make me feel happy, 's all.

JEANIE: Why dat going make you happy?

MANNY: Why you asking me all dese questions? You tink you my mud- dah or wat?

JEANIE: Why you no can be happy in Honolulu like everybody else? Maybe someting wrong wit' you. How come dey wen' fire you at da cannery?

MANNY: Aeh, I bust my ass dere and fo' wat? Only make da haole com- pany rich. Dey get da money and I stay poor. You see wat I mean?

JEANIE: Not everybody can be rich. Some people gotta be poor.

MANNY: You gotta be poor, not me.

JEANIE: If you like be rich, why you neva study some more? Why you neva go University Hawaii? Nobody stopping you.

MANNY: Shit, Jeanie, now you sounding like my muddah.

(She kisses him full on the mouth.)

JEANIE: Your muddah kiss you li'dat?

MANNY: Aeh, no talk dirty, eh.

JEANIE: Well, no call me your muddah.

MANNY: I neva call you my muddah. I said you sound like her. "Why you no go school, you no shame o' wat?"

JEANIE: Your muddah no talk li'dat.

MANNY: 'S wat you tink, you dunno nuttin'.

JEANIE: I wish I was more smart. Den you no take me so cheap.

MANNY: Yeah, I betta look around fo' one girl wit' good head.

(She whacks him on the arm.)

MANNY: You see wat I mean. Wat da hell you hit me fo'? And clean up da way you talk, eh, you sound like one guy.

JEANIE: Yeah? I look like one guy too?

(She shows off a nice pair of legs.)

MANNY: Yeah.

JEANIE: Wat you mean, yeah?

(JEANIE jumps on him, and they wrestle playfully on the ground. Now she's on top of him.)

You give up?

MANNY: Yeah, you too strong fo' me.

JEANIE: Okay. Now you not going Mainland, right?

MANNY: Not wen you stay on top of me li'dis.

JEANIE: Good. Den I not moving.

MANNY: Right now, you remind me of one girl I used to know.

JEANIE: Wat her name?

MANNY: You dunno her. She went away befo' you came here.

JEANIE: She look like me?

MANNY: Nah, she was betta looking.

(She hits him and gets off.)

MANNY: She always rub me da wrong way, just like you.

JEANIE: Oh yeah? I neva hear you complaining last night.

MANNY: I wonda wat she doing now. She went to da Mainland.

JEANIE: And wat? You like look her up? Forget it. She probably one whore by now.

MANNY: Aeh, no give whores bad name, eh. I used to know one wen I was one kid afta da war.

JEANIE: Bull lie.

MANNY: Fo' real. I used to hang out around Hotel Street shining shoes fo' da GIs. Dey give me tips like quarters, half-dollars, even dollar bills. And I always bring home da money to my muddah. I used to make her real happy da way I wen' try help even though I was just one kid. (OLDER MANNY is remembering too.)

OLDER MANNY: I had my own territory. If one nodda kid try come take my business, I hadda fight 'um off. My territory was my territory. Nobody can horn in, dat was it.

JEANIE: So wat about da whore?

MANNY and OLDER MANNY: Yeah, dis whore on Hotel Street was real nice to me. Once she even sew one button on my shirt. She wen' smile wen she finish. And she always like sing dis song to me. (The two MANNYs sing "Manuela Boy," strumming ukes.) Funny, yeah, how you no fo'get some tings.

JEANIE: 'S all?

MANNY: Wat mo' you like?

JEANIE: I tought you going say she wen' take you to bed.

MANNY: Aeh, I was only ten years old dat time. Even dey get deir rules. 'S da trouble wit' you, you tink all whores bad. Dey okay, da good ones okay.

JEANIE: I no care, Mista Expert, I gotta go work.

MANNY: Aeh, you tink Hank need one extra pin boy?

JEANIE: Who, you?

MANNY: Yeah.

JEANIE: You can do betta dan dat.

MANNY: Rememba wen I wen' bowl da two-seventy game?

JEANIE: Yeah, you wen' step on dog shit dat day.

MANNY: Nah, 's da time I wen' beat up da guy who was giving you trouble.

JEANIE: Yeah. Everybody at da bowling alley was scared of him.

MANNY: Bet you neva notice me till den, eh?

JEANIE: I saw you right away. I no stand behind da counta and just dream, you know. I was watching you all da time. I always tought you was diff'rent from da odda guys. More serious, more smart. Except da first time I wen' meet you.

MANNY: Why? Wat I did?

JEANIE: You wen' rent bowling shoes from me and you hadda ask if I had extra pair clean socks cause you wen' come in slippers.

MANNY: Sure. Damn shoes was sticky inside. No can tell wat kine guys wen' wear 'um befo' me. You like I get VD feet or wat? Here, I give you someting.

(He slides a bare foot up JEANIE's leg.)

JEANIE: Aeh, watch it. I no like your stink toe jams.

(She screams and runs off in mock horror with MANNY right behind her.)

OLDER MANNY: Dat was one sweet time wit' Jeanie. She was one tarrific girl. She deserved one betta guy dan me.

(Lights change. It is late afternoon. BEAR enters, sits on the ground and examines his toes carefully, one at a time. MANNY enters, OLDER MANNY joins the two.)

MANNY: Aeh, Bear, you trying to count to twenty?

BEAR: No, I was tinking how come my toes so crooked. Look ugly, eh?

MANNY: You know wat dey say: crooked toes, crooked prick.

BEAR: Aeh, bull lie, who said dat? Sheila?

MANNY: Sheila? Wat, you fooling around wit' her?

BEAR: Maybe. Why? Wassamadda wit' Sheila?

MANNY: She too hairy. Why you no tell her shave her legs?

BEAR: Her faddah no let her.

MANNY: She get mo' hair on her legs dan you.

(BEAR pulls up a pants leg and admires his leg.)

BEAR: Yeah, I get nice legs, eh?

MANNY: Real bow-legged. Like one horseshoe.

BEAR: Jealous bugga.

(BEAR spots an ant on the ground.)

Aeh, look, see dat ant? All by himself. Where you tink he going?

MANNY: He going visit his girlfriend, tell her shave her legs.

BEAR: He coming dis way.

MANNY: Watch dis.

(MANNY puts a hand down to block the ant.)

BEAR: Now he going da odda way.

(MANNY puts his other hand down to thwart the ant again.)

MANNY: If ants can shit, he shitting right now. Look at him, back and
fort', round and round. He dunno wat fo' do, everyting crowding in
on him so fast.

BEAR: I like try someting.

(BEAR spits at the ant but hits MANNY's hand.)

MANNY: Aeh, who tell you spit on my hand.

BEAR: Sorry, eh. I like circle him wit' spit so he no can escape.

(He spits again and again.)

MANNY: Now look wat you did. You spit right on him.

BEAR: No can help, he wen' run right unda my spit, da dumb ant.

MANNY: Now da bugga drowning in your spit.

BEAR: He lucky dog shit neva fall on him.

MANNY: He getting weak.

BEAR: Little bit mo' and ma-ke, die, dead.

(MANNY finds a rusty nail and uses it to lift the ant out of the spit.)

BEAR: He dead?

MANNY: No.

*(Offstage a string of firecrackers goes off. CABRAL and CHAMP run in
laughing.)*

Dat was you guys wit' da firecrackas?

CABRAL: Yeah. Loud, eh.

BEAR: You guys dumb. You like da cops come afta you?

CHAMP: Wat we care? We just tell 'um you wen' light 'um.

BEAR: Yeah? I light up your nose first.

CHAMP: See dis firecracka?

*(CHAMP pretends to light it, then quickly shoves it down BEAR's pants.
BEAR jumps up and down yelling, but there is no pop.)*

BEAR: You crazy or wat? Wat if wen' explode?

CHAMP: Den you go around talking like *(falsetto)* Mickey Mouse.

BEAR: You crazy, you know dat. Dey betta lock you up in Kaneohe. Aeh,
Cabral, why you hang around one crazy guy like him fo'?

CABRAL: I helping him train, man, wat you tink. You see here da next
middleweight champion of da world. Show 'um your stuff, Champ.

(CHAMP shadow-boxes.)

Dere's a left, anodda left, and a right, and he's down. Da crowd is going wild! *(Makes sound of roaring crowd.)* Da winna and new champion!

(CABRAL raises CHAMP's arm in triumph, and both jump around yelling and prancing joyously.)

BEAR *(to CABRAL)*: Shit, you just as crazy as him.

CHAMP: Manny, we go down Maunakea Street buy some manapuas.

MANNY: Nah, I not hungry.

CABRAL: Wat about you, Bear, you hungry?

CHAMP: Wat kine question dat? You know he hungry, he always hungry, you tell me wen he not hungry.

BEAR: Aeh, wait, maybe I get full stomach now. I wen' just eat saimin, laulau, and kalua pig, so no talk unless you know. Chee, some guys!

CABRAL: Okay, so you no like nuttin', eh?

BEAR: Get me t'ree manapuas.

CHAMP: See wat I told you.

MANNY: Aeh, da ant moving.

CHAMP: Wat dat, one red ant? Lemme step on 'um.

MANNY: Watch it!

BEAR: Give 'um room, you guys, give 'um room!

CABRAL: Wat so special about dat ant?

BEAR: Dis ant one tough bugga.

CABRAL: I like cacaroach betta. You know, da big fat kine wit' da long feelas. And I like step on 'um and squish 'um so all da guts come out. And he still alive wen he crawling away dragging his guts wit' him.

BEAR: Aeh, fo'get my manapuas. I no feel like eat now.

MANNY: Okay, da ant wen' in da crack.

BEAR: Good. Now he can go home and tell his family wat wen' happen. Da bugga betta watch out fo' da spit next time. No can trust nobody or nuttin' around here.

CHAMP: I tink you guys stay in da alley too long, no nuff sun, make da head mushy, know wat I mean?

BEAR: You da one wit' da mushy head, you punch-drunk already.

CHAMP: C'mon, c'mon, brah, I take you on right now.

BEAR: Big deal, big deal, damn ant get mo' balls dan you.

CHAMP: You had it already. 'S it, brah.

BEAR: I like see you try someting. Go 'head, c'mon, c'mon, try, try, make me scared, make me cry, aeh, aeh, aeh, go, man.

(*BEAR shows some fancy but amateurish footwork.*)

Aeh, Manny, tarrific, eh.

MANNY: Shaka, just like Dado Marino.

CHAMP: Shit, you look like one mahu dancing on Beretania.

BEAR: Aeh, Cabral, see how jealous him?

CABRAL: You betta look out, Bear, he in tarrific shape now.

BEAR: Bull lie. He no can catch me. Aeh, Champ, come kiss my okole.

(*BEAR bends over and moons CHAMP.*)

CHAMP: I ready fo' some roadwork.

(*BEAR exits laughing.*)

Aeh, I coming afta you, you fat ass bugga!

(*CHAMP and CABRAL go off in the chase. Lights go down on the scene and up on MAMA in the kitchen area sorting out laundry. She wears a waitress uniform of white blouse and black skirt. OLDER MANNY moves on the edge of the scene. MANNY enters. It is dusk.*)

MAMA: Where Jojo?

MANNY: How da hell I know? Maybe he stay A'ala Park playing ball.

MAMA: You sure? You his big bruddah, you gotta take care of him.

MANNY: No worry about Jojo. You treat him like one kid, 's why no good. He too soft. He gotta be tough live around here. Leave 'um alone little while, let 'um get in trouble if he like.

MAMA: I no like Jojo turn out like you. He get chance go university and be somebody. Not like you.

MANNY: Yeah, yeah, I know. You told me million times already. Too late fo' me, 's how you feel. But someday I going make plenny money my way and I make sure Jojo go school all he like. No worry about dat. If 's wat you like, I make sure he go.

MAMA: You get smart mout', 's all, 's why no good. Wen you was one kid, you was mo' betta. Now you only know how play ukulele, waste time. I wish you was mo' . . .

MANNY: Wat? Wat? Tell me, tell me . . .

OLDER MANNY: Wat you like, Mama, tell me wat you wish. If I know, maybe I can make your wish come—

MAMA: Neva mind. You just like Papa.

MANNY: Wat you mean?

MAMA: Only know how to play.

MANNY: Papa was okay.

MAMA: He was one drunkard.

MANNY: He neva can help dat.

MAMA: I waste my time on him.

MANNY: He was going change, I know dat. I rememba. If he neva die, maybe . . .

MAMA: Yeah, he fool you. You was one kid, wat you know. He was weak, just like you.

MANNY: Wat you mean, weak. I not weak. Jojo da one weak. Jojo da one no can do nuttin'. I can do anyting I like.

MAMA: Talk, talk, talk, just like Papa.

MANNY: Why you keep reminding me of him?

MAMA: Because every time I look at you, I see Papa.

(She puts away the laundry.)

I gotta go work. I get leftovas in da icebox. You can warm up fo' Jojo and you tonight.

MANNY: Jojo can warm up his own kaukau.

(MANNY exits. MAMA doesn't realize this.)

OLDER MANNY: Wat went wrong, Mama? 'S wat I like know. Wat I did to make you mad at me? I get so many questions, so few answers.

MAMA: Manny, I know you hate me because I scold you so much. I dunno why I do dat. I cannot help myself. All my fault. Someday I going make it up to you.

(She turns to see MANNY is gone.)

OLDER MANNY: No, Mama, I gotta make it up to you. But how?

(Lights down on kitchen as MAMA exits. Lights up on JOJO as he enters with a softball.)

JOJO: Aeh, Manny, catch.

(He throws to MANNY, who catches the ball.)

MANNY: Wat you was doing all dis time, playing in da park? You no can just play all da time. No fool around. You gotta study.

JOJO: Manny, no mo' school now. No start till Septemba.

MANNY: I know dat. You tink I dumb or wat? You can still study, go library, read books, da kine stuff. No screw around like one stupid kid.

JOJO: You mad at me, Manny? I wen' do someting? I neva mean . . . wat I did?

MANNY: Nuttin', nuttin', you neva do nuttin'. 'S okay, no worry. Wat you going do if I not here?

JOJO: Why? You going Mainland?

MANNY: Yeah. Time to go up and hit it big. I get chance on da Mainland. Not like here.

JOJO: Wat you going do dere?

MANNY: Hell, man, maybe I going drive in da Indianapolis Five Hundred and win da first prize, wit' one trophy dis big. And dey going pour da champagne ova me, and da beauty queen going give me one vic'try kiss. Going taste real sweet, man.

JOJO: Yeah, I going brag to all my friends, "My bruddah da fastest race driva in da world."

MANNY: And I going make one big pile of money on da Mainland. Den I can take care of Mama.

(OLDER MANNY *sits next to* JOJO.)

JOJO: If Papa was wit' us, he can enjoy all dat too.

MANNY: Da old man really knew how to enjoy himself. He had lotta friends, you know, always talking story wit' dem. I tink 's wat he like doing da best. Too bad you neva know him.

JOJO: Yeah, I wish he wen' live mo' long.

MANNY: He used to like drink, but he was one happy drunk. Some guys wen dey drink, dey get mean. Not da old man. Wen he was drunk, he was happy, singing songs, talking to me. In fact, da only time he really talk to me was wen he was drunk. So sometimes I used to wish he drink so he can fo'get and be happy. Funny, eh. Wen he ask me, I used to sneak down to da Sakura Bar back door and buy some liquor fo' him. Da owner felt sorry fo' him, I guess.

OLDER MANNY: Manny, I tink da owner just wanted to make a few bucks on da side. Everybody look out for demselves. Who knows. You tink da old man was a happy drunk? But drunk is drunk, right?

JOJO: Why da old man had to drink?

MANNY: Some guys just get da taste in da mout' and pau. Wen he worked at da cannery, he used to repair da machines. I hear he was good.

OLDER MANNY: I hear he was good wit' da wahines too, Manny. No fo'get dat. Fool around on da side, no problem, eh. So long as Mama dunno, no harm, eh.

MANNY: I gotta find one job so I can save enough money to go to da Mainland. Den I can show Mama.

JOJO: Ma's birt'day coming up. I bought her one present.

MANNY: Her birt'day? Where you wen' get da money?

JOJO: Working at da market.

MANNY: I tought you give dat money to Mama?

JOJO: Yeah, most of dem, but I wen' save little bit from dat. I going tell her da present from you and me.

MANNY: Wat you wen' get her?

JOJO: Handkerchiefs.

MANNY: Handkerchiefs? No mo' betta stuff dan dat?

JOJO: I dunno. Wat? Perfume?

MANNY: She no need perfume.

JOJO: Wat you tink she like?

MANNY: Da handkerchiefs okay. 'S betta dan nuttin'. Someday we can buy her da expensive kine stuff.

JOJO: Wen we come millionaires, eh?

MANNY: Yeah, wen we come millionaires.

JOJO: How long going take us for be millionaires?

MANNY: 'Bout hundred years.

JOJO: Dat long? 'S too long, Manny. Five years maybe.

MANNY: Yeah, five years.

JOJO: Den we can buy one big white house just like da kine da haoles get.

MANNY: One big two-story house wit' t'ree bedrooms, one fo' you, one fo' Mama and one fo' me. Den we no need share da bat'room wit' odda people like now.

JOJO: Wat about one swimming pool?

MANNY: Fo' wat? You can go Waikiki Beach swim.

JOJO: I know. But I like one pool too, just like in da movies.

MANNY: You no going get someting fo' Mama?

JOJO: Oh yeah. We go get her one nice, big, white stove. Good, eh? And one new washing machine and—

MANNY: Da kine stuff okay, but we can hire people to do dat. We gotta get her some new clothes, right?

JOJO: Yeah, da real expensive kine, da kine da haoles wear. Wat you like, Manny?

MANNY: Me? I not fussy. I take one white Cadillac wit' all da trimmings. And one yacht fo' go deep-sea fishing. And you know wat I like catch? One giant shark.

JOJO: One shark! Yeah! Da mout' dis big and he like swallow us up.

MANNY: But we get da uppa hand, see, so da bugga no mo' chance. We get our hook in him and he fighting and fighting, but in da end, he give up, he lose and we win. And we lift him outta da ocean and wow going stretch up to da sky almost. Aeh, da newspapers gotta take our picture togedda 'cause we wen' catch da biggest shark in da whole world.

JOJO: Hmmm, nice to dream, yeah.

MANNY: Wat you mean, dream? Dat ain't no dream, man, you wait. Someday, someday, all dat going come true. Wassamadda, you no believe me?

JOJO: I believe you, Manny.

MANNY: Yeah, den I can take Mama away from here, to one nice, clean and happy place.

(Lights down on MANNY *and* JOJO *as they exit.* OLDER MANNY *remains on the stage. Lights up on kitchen with* MAMA *and* SLICK, *who is shirtless. He's kissing her but she stops him.)*

MAMA: You betta go befo' da boys come home.

SLICK: Wat you worry fo'?

MAMA: I no like dey see you.

SLICK: You shame of me o' wat?

MAMA: Hurry up. Jojo said dey was going to da Princess Theatre. Wat if dey come home early?

*(*OLDER MANNY *watches, yet often looks away.)*

Mo' betta dis way. Dey no undastand.

SLICK: You know wen I first see you in da cafe, I knew you was hungry, hungry fo' one good—

MAMA: Shhhh, no talk li'dat.

(She gives him his shirt, which he puts on. MANNY *enters and stands far away watching.)*

SLICK: Yeah, you act so quiet, but inside you just like one volcano. No need hide how you feel. You lonesome, you not one machine. You need some loving to keep you young.

MAMA: Wen my husband was alive, I neva do nuttin' behind his back. I neva do dis kine . . .

SLICK: Aeh, I know, I know. You not dat kine wahine. Wat we did was natural, you know, man and woman, nuttin' wrong wit' dat.

MAMA: Mo' betta I no see you again.

SLICK: Honey, you someting special. Know wat I mean? I get around wit' da wahines, 's no secret. But I tell you right now, I neva get one good as you. Fo' real. Da odda girls, dey kinna low class, but not you. You one hot dish. Wen I going see you again?

MAMA: I busy.

SLICK: Tomorrow?

MAMA: I dunno.

SLICK: You know wat? I no mo' cigarettes. You can lend me few bucks? I gotta get some packs.

(She searches in her purse.)

MAMA: Here, only couple dollars.

SLICK: 'S good enough. I going be tinking about you tonight. Yeah, I gotta see you some mo'. Aeh, no worry, we good togedda. I feel like going wit' you again, right now.

MAMA: Go, go. Make sure nobody see you.

SLICK: Okay, okay, baby.

(SLICK leaves with a smug smile. He walks downstage and lights a cigarette. MANNY stalks his prey in the shadows. He takes out a switchblade knife, clicks it open. The blade glistens. MANNY circles SLICK like a panther. OLDER MANNY is at his side, also coiled to strike. MANNY now jumps SLICK from behind.)

SLICK: Wat, wat? Aeh, wat you like? No do nuttin', no do nuttin'.

(MANNY flashes the knife at SLICK's face.)

MANNY: You know wat I like, Slick?

SLICK: I dunno, I dunno. Who you?

MANNY: You know, no act dumb.

SLICK: No, no, wait, I no mo' money.

MANNY: I no like your fucking money. I like your blood.

SLICK: I neva do nuttin'.

MANNY: No lie to me, you bastard. I going make sure you no do nuttin' again.

SLICK: Wait, wait! Gimme chance. No kill me.

MANNY: I not going kill you. 'S too easy. I going cut off your balls and prick and stuff 'um in your mout'. How you like dat, eh, sound good to you?

SLICK: No, no, no.

MANNY: You tink I blind o' wat? I see you around. I know your style wit' da wahines. Now you going feel my style.

SLICK: No, no, okay, wait, I not going see her again. Lemme go, lemme go, please!

MANNY: Yeah, beg, you fucka, beg!

(He puts the blade at SLICK's *groin.)*

SLICK: Aaaaahhhhh, aaaaaahhhhhh, aaahhhhhh . . .

*(*SLICK *sags like a bag of potatoes, helpless in panic, and slips to the ground.* MANNY *kicks him in the stomach.* OLDER MANNY *adds two more kicks.)*

MANNY: Go 'head, crawl, you bastard. Crawl, crawl!

OLDER MANNY: If I see you near her again, I going cut you up so bad, you going beg me to kill you.

*(*SLICK *drags himself across the floor and exits. Lights down on the alley, lights up on kitchen.* MAMA *is wearing a simple summer dress.* JOJO *enters with a little gift. It is night.)*

JOJO: Mama, dis for you. Your birt'day present. See, me and Manny neva fo'get. Go open 'um.

*(*MANNY *enters with* OLDER MANNY *right behind.)*

MAMA: Why you do dis fo'?

JOJO: Well, nuttin' special but—

MAMA: I no need present.

(She opens the gift box and takes out the handkerchiefs.)

Oh nice. I can make good use.

JOJO: Yeah, 's wat we tought. Me and Manny.

MAMA: T'ank you, Jojo.

JOJO: Manny too.

MAMA: T'ank you, Manny. Nice present.

JOJO: Mama, wen Manny and me get rich, we going buy you betta stuff. 'S right, eh, Manny?

*(*MANNY *doesn't answer. There's an awkward silence.)*

JOJO: I get one mo' surprise. Wait, eh. I neva even tell Manny.

*(*JOJO *exits.)*

MAMA: I wonda wat Jojo—

MANNY: I saw you.

MAMA: Wat?

MANNY: I know wat you was doing.

MAMA: Wat you mean? Why you acting so funny?

MANNY: I know, I know.

MAMA: Wat you getting mad fo'? Wat you talking?

MANNY: You neva fool me. I saw you wit' da bastard.

MAMA: Jojo going hear you.

MANNY: I saw you.

MAMA: Shut up, no talk, Jojo.

(JOJO enters with a small cake and one lighted candle.)

You spend money on cake too?

JOJO: No. I was telling Mrs. Chong at da bakery was your birt'day, so she wen' give me dis cake free. One day old, she said, but still good. You gotta blow out da candle and make your wish. C'mon, Mama.

(She blows out the candle.)

Okay, You wen' make your wish?

(MAMA looks at MANNY.)

MAMA: Yes.

JOJO: Good. Now no tell me or Manny 'cause den not going come true.

(MANNY exits.)

JOJO: Cut da cake, Mama. Wassamadda, you crying?

MAMA: No.

JOJO: Why you crying?

MAMA: Oh, you make me happy, 's why.

(She hugs JOJO, who's embarrassed, so he wiggles away to sit on a chair.)

JOJO: Slice up da cake, Mama. I like one big piece.

(Lights down on the kitchen. Lights up on another part of the stage as MANNY sits with his back against the wall. OLDER MANNY sits next to MANNY.)

MANNY: I gotta get out.

OLDER MANNY: Go, go. Run away now befo' too late. No wait fo' nuttin'. If you go now—

MANNY: Where da hell I can go? I no mo' enough money to go Mainland. And I gotta watch Jojo, make sure he no take da wrong road. If

I no stay, da kid going get in trouble, I know dat. And I gotta keep my eye on dat bum Slick. I shoulda cut off his balls.

OLDER MANNY: Da bugga no mo' guts, he not going show his face around here again. We wen' take good care of him.

MANNY: Wat about odda guys? If I stay Mainland, dey going come around and try use her like one . . .

OLDER MANNY: Wat? You going be her watchdog?

MANNY: I no like guys take her cheap. She dunno about da kine guys. Next ting you know, dey like move in and take ova. Make her work and spend her money.

OLDER MANNY: I know. But wat if she no like we protect her? Wat if she lonesome fo' one guy who make her feel like one woman and not like one muddah?

MANNY: And how da guy going treat Jojo? Beat 'um up? Chase 'um outta da house? Jojo one good kid, he going suffa and I not going be around.

OLDER MANNY: 'S why hard.

(MANNY *walks off, leaving* OLDER MANNY *alone.* SLICK *enters. He lights a cigarette, looks around nervously. He paces slowly, looking left and right, waiting.* OLDER MANNY *circles him.* SLICK *senses a presence; an uneasy feeling overcomes him. He drops the cigarette and smashes it with his slipper.* MANNY *returns and quietly draws up to* SLICK.)

SLICK: Wat da hell she doing? She betta hurry up and come befo' I get mad.

MANNY: Wat you doing?

SLICK: Huh?

MANNY: Who you waiting fo'?

SLICK: Nobody.

MANNY: You get one cigarette?

OLDER MANNY: I like one smoke.

(SLICK *nervously offers one from his pack.*)

MANNY: You no mo' Lucky Strike?

OLDER MANNY: LSMFT, Lucky Strike Means Fine Tobacco.

SLICK: 'S all I get.

MANNY: Aaahhh, wat good you? Lucky Strike da best. You know wat, you can lend me few bucks?

SLICK: I no get too much.

OLDER MANNY: You get enough.

MANNY: Oh, I no like leave you wit' one empty pocket, but I gotta get my Lucky Strike. If I no get wat I like, I get pissed off and den, I dunno, I go liddle bit pupule. Know wat I mean?

(MANNY jerks suddenly and SLICK jumps back.)

Wat? Wassamadda? Someting wrong?

SLICK: No.

MANNY: You know, I tought you promise you not going stick around here. I tought maybe you going move to Maui o' Big Island o' da Mainland.

SLICK: No mo' money go da kine place.

MANNY: You eva see Alaska? I hear da place real nice. Wat you tink? You like go?

SLICK: If I get da cash.

OLDER MANNY: She coming, Manny. I can see her.

MANNY: Somebody going give you da dough?

SLICK: No.

MANNY: No lie to me. 'S one ting I no like. I hate guys who fucking lie to me.

SLICK: Not me, not me.

MANNY: Try wait. No move. I going be right ova dere.

(MANNY moves into the shadows. OLDER MANNY looks offstage and backs away as MAMA enters and goes to SLICK.)

MAMA: I told you I coming.

SLICK: Wat?

MAMA: Dis all da money I can give you.

SLICK: Wat?

MAMA: Dis wat you wanted. Take 'um.

(She shoves an envelope in his hands.)

SLICK: Wat dis?

MAMA: No act dumb. You wen' ask fo' da money. Now, go away. Pau. No bodda me. I wen' make one mistake. My boy Manny know about you. If he find out about dis, he going kill you. So you betta watch out and run away.

(MAMA leaves. MANNY returns.)

MANNY: You rich now, eh. Get plenny money in dere?

SLICK: Dis not fo' me.

(He gives the envelope to MANNY.)

MANNY: You sure? She wen' give 'um to you, not me.

SLICK: I neva ask fo' da money.

MANNY: I told you I no like guys lie to me. Da guys call you Slick, because you wen' give 'um to you, not me.

SLICK: I neva ask fo' da money.

MANNY: I told you I no like guys lie to me. Da guys call you Slick, because you one real slicka, eh?

SLICK: No.

MANNY: You neva learn your lesson from last time, eh, Slick, you still looking fo' mo' trouble.

SLICK (*cowering*): Not me.

MANNY: Man, I need one smoke right now. How 'bout it? You going lend me some bucks fo' my Lucky Strikes?

(*SLICK takes out his wallet and hands him the cash.*)

SLICK: 'S all I get.

MANNY: Chee, you real nice guy, eh. You going lend me all dis?

SLICK: Yeah.

MANNY: Cigarettes costing mo' and mo' nowdays. You really helping me out.

(*MANNY crowds SLICK into a corner.*)

SLICK: No kill me, I . . . I . . .

MANNY: I going say dis to you one mo' time, so listen real good. I no like see your fucking face again. Go as far away as you can as fast as you can. If I can smell you, I coming afta you. And dat going be da last day of your life. Undastand?

SLICK: I going, I going . . .

(*MANNY makes a move to strike him, and SLICK sinks to the ground and rolls himself up into a ball.*)

OLDER MANNY: Get da fuck outta here! Go befo' I kill you, you sonavabitch!

(*SLICK scrambles out on his hands and knees. JEANIE enters from the opposite direction.*)

JEANIE: Da bowling alley was busy tonight. You should bowl some mo'. You can be one professional. Hank said all you gotta do is practice. He said you good now, but if you practice hard, you can be one expert. You listening to me?

MANNY: Yeah.

JEANIE: No lie. Why you so quiet? I was tinking about taking one job at Bowl-O-Drome. Good chance for me. But den how you feel if I move to McCully side. . . . Or else I like go Honolulu Business College, study and be one secretary or someting. I can go night school. Which you tink betta? If I go HBC, I no need move from here. Going take me two years to finish. Wat you tink I should do?

MANNY: You know your life betta dan me.

JEANIE: But I like know how you feel.

MANNY: I dunno. 'S up to you.

JEANIE: You no care wat I do?

MANNY: Sure I care. I like you be happy. If I can help you, I go fo' broke. But wat I can do fo' you? Nuttin'. Only way I can take care of you is make sure nobody give you trouble. . . . I was tinking if I can move in wit' you.

JEANIE: Why? Someting happen?

MANNY: Too crowded wit' Jojo and my muddah dere. Was one mistake go back anyway. If I neva lose my job, I can keep my own place.

JEANIE: You can live wit' me, you know dat.

MANNY: My faddah neva can hold down one job, but not his fault.

OLDER MANNY: No make excuses fo' da old man, Manny.

MANNY: Was da haole bosses, dey wen' fire him.

OLDER MANNY: Because he neva can hold his liquor. Wat can do if you fall asleep at work because you drink too much? Dey could smell da liquor on his breath.

MANNY: 'S wat my faddah used to tell me, so I know. Damn haoles neva give a damn about us local people. Dey always tink we too stupid and dey so smart.

OLDER MANNY: Da old man always lied to you. He was one damn good liar. And you was just one kid, wat you know about life? Da old man wen' poison your head.

MANNY: My faddah had lotta jobs. And wen people ask, I used to lie, tell 'um he wen' quit wen dey fired him.

OLDER MANNY: You know how my faddah wen' die?

MANNY: Somebody wen' knife da old man in da alley. Right here, where us guys hang out.

JEANIE: Wen?

OLDER MANNY: I was about eight o' nine. Dat night he neva come home yet, so my muddah told me to go find him and bring him home.

MANNY: I neva like do dat because I know dey going fight again.

OLDER MANNY: I went to da Sakura Bar first, den I saw him lying in da alley, on his stomach.

MANNY: Right away I can smell da liquor. Stink. Da bugga was drunk again.

OLDER MANNY: And I tought, shit, if I bring him home dey only going fight again and broke stuff. So I wen' leave him dere. See, I neva know about da knifing. I tought he was just drunk.

MANNY: Instead of dragging him home, I went to A'ala Park and I wen' sleep in da bandstand dat night. See, I neva know he was bleeding. If I know, I help him.

JEANIE: Nobody can blame you.

MANNY: I neva tell nobody about dis. Not even my muddah. Was her fault anyway.

JEANIE: Not your muddah fault. She one nice lady.

MANNY: You dunno wat you talking. See, my muddah neva treat him right. If she was mo' nice to him, den I know he no drink so much. But she was always on his ass squawking about dis o' dat.

OLDER MANNY: And wat about da times he used to slap Mama around?

MANNY: He neva can take da nagging, too much, too much nag, nag, nag. He neva can take it. If she was good to him, den dat night I bring him home right away. Because of her, he wen' bleed to death.

JEANIE: Your poor muddah. She had lotta trouble.

MANNY: You neva hear nuttin' I said?

OLDER MANNY: I hear, I hear. My whole life I keep hearing you. Sometimes you broke my ears listening to everyting in your head. Damn, I wish I can poke around in dere. I bet da gears all rusty. Nuttin' working right.

JEANIE: I just trying to explain to you—

MANNY: 'S da trouble wit' you, you no listen. You tink I lying to you? You tink I lying like my faddah? You just like my muddah, you only like give me bad time. Wen my old man like tell my muddah someting, she always make him sound like he stupid. Wat he can do? Mo' betta get drunk.

(OLDER MANNY stands and becomes Papa. MANNY covers his ears.)

OLDER MANNY: Where Manny? Get my damn stick. Where da hell da fucking ting? Go get 'um. I gotta whip your fucking ass, you dumb kid. I tell you all da time, no come bodda me at da bar. How you tink I feel, everybody looking at me? You tink good fun? *(Makes striking motions with imaginary stick)* Eh! Eh! Eh! You like dat? You can feel how mad I stay? You no fo'get dis, you fucking rotten shit!

(OLDER MANNY slumps to the ground.)

JEANIE: Maybe your faddah was weak.

MANNY: Wat you mean, weak? He neva was weak, he was . . . he was . . . Why you no can keep your mout' shut? You make me sick.

JEANIE: You make me sick too. Maybe you just like your faddah. Maybe 's why your muddah get mad at you every time.

MANNY: Shaddup!

(He slaps her across the face. She is stunned for a second, then runs off angrily.)

OLDER MANNY: Da old man ma-ke long time ago but he still causing trouble, yeah. How old we was, Manny? Eh? Eight? Nine? How come da old man drink so much? Rememba, he used to come up and say: "Aeh, everybody, dis my boy Manny. Aeh, Manny, how you? You good boy, eh, Manny? Aeh, I love dis boy, you know. Yeah, he going be one big man someday. Big shot! You know why? You know? 'Cause he my boy, he just like me, he my blood, 's why."

(The two MANNYs face the audience in the following exchange. Circles of light focus on them.)

MANNY: Pop, we go home.

OLDER MANNY: Why?

MANNY: People laughing at you.

OLDER MANNY: Me? Wat fo'? Dey not laughing. Dey my friends.

MANNY: Dey laughing behind your back. Dey no care about you.

OLDER MANNY: Sure, dey care, dey my friends. I get plenny friends. You ask dem.

MANNY: We go already. Late.

OLDER MANNY: Nah, nah, nah, time fo' fun and drink. Yeah, yeah, I buy drinks fo' you guys, no worry, old Joe take care his buddies.

MANNY: Mama going get mad if I no bring you home.

OLDER MANNY: Who? Mama? Wassamadda, you mama's boy? Eh? I get one mama's boy?

MANNY: No.

OLDER MANNY: Wat you said? I neva hear. Tell me wat, eh, wat?

MANNY: I said no.

OLDER MANNY: Fucking mama's boy, 's you. I wish you was one real boy, one real son, not one mama's boy.

MANNY: I said I not one mama's boy.

OLDER MANNY: Aeh, no get sassy wit' me. You like one slap. Eh? Eh? I give one . . . *(A slapping motion and* MANNY *feels it.)* How dat feel? Good, eh? You raise your voice to me, your faddah, I give you one good slap and one mo' and one mo'. At least I get one mo' boy, Jojo, he da one my boy, you mama's boy.

MANNY: Why you no shut up? Why you no just go away and no come back? Why you no just ma-ke? Die! I wish you was dead!

*(*MANNY *exits.)*

OLDER MANNY *(as himself)* : Ma-ke . . . die . . . dead.

(Lights up slowly on alley. It is day. BEAR *comes out of the pool hall's back door with* UJI*.)*

BEAR: Dey make Hawai'i one state today? 'S wat da radio said?

UJI: Yeah. Too good, eh.

BEAR: Aeh, statehood no big deal. I no feel diff'rent today from yesta-day.

UJI: We gotta celebrate.

BEAR: 'S why you wen' bring out da dry akule and lomi lomi salmon fo' everybody?

UJI: Sure, now we first-class American citizens.

*(*JOJO *enters with a small American flag.)*

JOJO: Look, dis flag get fifty stars.

BEAR: You sure?

JOJO: Yeah, try count 'um.

*(*BEAR *starts counting but stops.)*

BEAR: Too much trouble. I take your word. How you get 'um?

JOJO: One man passing 'um out. Free.

BEAR: Aeh, I going see if I can get some mo'. Wait, eh.

(He exits quickly.)

JOJO: You wen' see Manny today?

UJI: No. Why, someting wrong?

JOJO: No, no. He neva come home last night, so . . .

UJI: Maybe he feel bad because no mo' job. Too bad da cannery wen' fire him.

JOJO: Oh no, dey neva do dat. He wen' quit because, ah, he can get one betta job in Waikiki. In one of da hotels, Royal Hawaiian, I tink.

UJI: Yeah? Das good. Manny lucky den.

JOJO: Yeah, Manny no fool around. He know wat he doing.

(BEAR *returns with one flag.*)

BEAR: Da guy out dere manini bugga. He get plenny flags but he give me only one. If I get da flags he get, I can make money selling 'um half-buck one. Jojo, you and me go out again and try get some mo' flags. Da mo' you can get, da mo' we can sell.

JOJO: 'S not legal, eh?

BEAR: No worry about legal. I handle da kine. We go. Aeh, Uji-san, we see you, eh, me and Jojo going make some money. Jojo, now I split da profits wit' you, okay? You just give 'um your innocent face and keep asking fo' flags. Wat we doing is patriotic, so no need sweat.

(*As they exit,* MANNY *and* JEANIE *enter from the opposite end.* OLDER MANNY *joins them.* UJI *doesn't see them right away, as he is busy smoking a cigarette.*)

MANNY: I dunno why I said dose tings last night. My head was so mess up. I neva mean to hit you.

JEANIE: Why you so scared of getting hurt? If you trust me, den I no feel so bad. But you neva listen to me. Sometimes I talking to you, and I know your mind is tousand miles away. I no can reach you li'dat.

MANNY: Afta last night, I went A'ala Park so nobody bodda me. You dunno da tings I get in my head, tings I gotta clear up.

JEANIE: Wat tings?

MANNY: You no can undastand. If you was one guy maybe but . . .

JEANIE: You see! You always say tings li'dat. Wat, because I one girl, I mo' stupid dan one man? You take me cheap, you know dat?

MANNY: Wat?

JEANIE: You take me cheap. You say mo' nice tings about whores.

MANNY: I dunno wat to say.

OLDER MANNY: Jeanie, I wish I wen' give you da love and undastanding you deserved. I neva appreciated you. I'm sorry.

(JEANIE *exits.* OLDER MANNY *strums his ukulele and sings one stanza of Queen Liliuokalani's song, "Sanoe." The last line of the stanza is repeated by the two* MANNYS. UJI *comes over.*)

UJI: Manny, Jojo was looking fo' you. He was worried.

MANNY: About wat?

UJI: He said you neva come home.

MANNY: Nah, dat was nuttin'.

UJI: He said you going work at Royal Hawaiian Hotel.

MANNY: Jojo said dat?

UJI: Good you going work dere.

MANNY: I dunno yet. I tink betta if I go Mainland.

UJI: Aaahhh, you no like go dere. Poho. Waste time.

MANNY: Get mo' chance on da Mainland.

UJI: No can beat Hawai'i. And now we get statehood.

MANNY: Wat statehood going do fo' me? Nuttin'.

UJI: Wat Mainland can do fo' you?

MANNY: Get forty-nine states to look fo' jobs.

UJI: Yeah but wat kine work you going do?

MANNY: Anyting betta dan da cannery.

UJI: I was like you wen I was young. I work on one freighta and sail to da Mainland. Was junk ova dere. Dose days was hard fo' guys like us. If you not haole, you hard luck.

MANNY: Ova here da same. Wat da diff'rence?

UJI: Maybe Mainland betta nowdays. But I still tink Hawai'i betta fo' people like us. We all stick togedda, no pilikia. Up dere, you going be all alone. I pity you.

(BEAR and JOJO reenter.)

JOJO: Dere Manny.

BEAR: No bodda him now. You no can see he busy? Okay, we get fourteen flags. We sell 'um fifty cents each, 's seven dollars. We split 'um even, four bucks fo' me, t'ree bucks fo' you.

JOJO: Aeh, 's not fair.

(MANNY and UJI enter the pool hall.)

BEAR: Was my idea, right?

JOJO: Yeah.

BEAR: I olda dan you, right?

JOJO: Yeah.

BEAR: I betta-looking dan you, right?

JOJO: No.

BEAR: No? Aeh, I still win two outta t'ree. Chee, Jojo, no make me feel bad. Okay, I get t'ree seventy-five, you get t'ree twenty-five. And no ask fo' mo' dan dat, or I sell you to da gypsies on Hotel Street.

JOJO: I not scared. Da gypsies my friend.

BEAR: Yeah, yeah, everybody your friend. Aeh, Jojo, wen da tourists come in on da Lurline, you like be partnas wit' me?

JOJO: Wat I gotta do?

BEAR: We go out in da ocean dive fo' da coins dey t'row from da boat.

JOJO: I no can swim dat good.

BEAR: Easy, brah. I put you on one rubba tire and you just wave at da tourists and tell 'um t'row some coins in fo' good luck. Den I dive fo' da money. Haoles love da kine shit. Okay, partna, we go down Hall Street side make some money.

(*UJI emerges from the back door.*)

UJI: Aeh, you guys, Tiny wen' just give me some pipi-kaula. You like eat?

BEAR: Yeah, man. Jojo, I tell you one ting. If you get choice between eating and working, always eat. We can catch da suckas later. Tiny, still inside?

UJI: Shooting pool wit' Manny.

BEAR (*head inside the door*): Aeh, Tiny, you fat shit, where you? You like challenge eight ball? You scared o' wat? Aeh, aeh, aeh, c'mon, c'mon! (*BEAR enters through the back door. UJI and JOJO follow. Lights go down to indicate night. MANNY enters with his uke and sits next to OLDER MANNY.*)

OLDER MANNY: Nighttime. 'S wen you can really tink. Let your toughts swim in your head backstroke nice and easy, yeah, yeah, feel good, eh, dreaming about how good tings going be wen your luck change. Gotta get good luck sometimes. 'S right, eh, Manny, 's wat you tinking. So easy to dream, yeah. And da dream is always betta dan da reality. Aeh, I know wat I talking about. Why you fill up Jojo's head wit' all da bullshit about da Mainland? Wat you did so far in your life, Manny? You can answer dat? You screwed up your life, but not your fault. 'S wat you always say, right?

(*BEAR and JOJO enter.*)

BEAR: Some guys just not patriotic. Shit, dey no like dish out measly fifty cents fo' one new American flag.

JOJO: Funny, yeah, we neva can sell nuttin'.

BEAR: I hope dis teach you one lesson, Jojo.

JOJO: Yeah, no go in business wit' you.

BEAR: Aeh, no be li'dat. Wait till da Lurline come in, we scoop up den. Manny, you like go to da beach tomorrow?

MANNY: Wat fo'? Sell your flags to da tourists?

BEAR: No, no. Pick up some coeds. Get plenny hot-looking wahines lying around on da beach, especially by Queen's Surf. You know wat we can do—tell da wahines us guys beachboys and we can show 'um how fo' surf.

MANNY: You dunno how surf.

BEAR: Chee, not my fault I no mo' balance. I tink because I get flat feet.

MANNY: Wit' luau feet li'dat, you no need one surfboard.

BEAR: You can see us guys catching da waves at Makaha?

(BEAR mimes riding a surfboard and performing some fancy footwork.)

C'mon, Manny! Jojo, easy, brah, c'mon, let's go!

(MANNY jumps on BEAR's back and they go through a tandem surfing act. JOJO joins the fun.)

JOJO: One big wave coming.

BEAR: Easy, brah, easy, no sweat!

MANNY: Go, man, go! All da way!

BEAR: Watch dis! Watch dis!

(He dances clumsily, arms flailing. MANNY stretches his arms out, head up.)

MANNY: Look out, man, look out, make room, make room!

JOJO: I catching da wave too! Aeh, look at me!

(The three guys are laughing and yelling as CABRAL and CHAMP enter, carrying a six-pack of beer bottles.)

CHAMP: Aeh, aeh, aeh, can hear you guys from da street.

CABRAL: Yeah, I tought you guys was killing somebody in here.

BEAR: About time you guys wen' come. Man, I was t'irsty fo' some beer.

CABRAL: Shut your mout'. You already get enough beer in you last ten years. *(CABRAL hands a bottle toward BEAR, then pulls it back. BEAR growls menacingly. CABRAL jumps back and tosses him a bottle.)* You like one, Jojo?

MANNY: He too young. I no like he drink yet.

BEAR: Chee, just like one faddah. Tarrific, yeah.

CABRAL: You know, if my old man get tough wit' my muddah and hit her, she run quick get da butcha knife and wave 'um in da air. Da old man get scared, man. He know she mean business. Da butcha knife is da real equiliza.

BEAR: Good your old lady get guts li'dat.

CHAMP: My old man always running around wit' some broad, da bugga.

CABRAL: Wat you moaning about? You do da same ting.

CHAMP: So wat? I still young, eh, I get excuse fo' wat I do.

CABRAL: Excuse nuttin'. Manny, I told Champ no fool around wit' Ruby befo' da amateur fight 'cause he going lose all da strength in his legs. But he wen' see Ruby and he get all hard up and—

BEAR: Aeh, wait. Jojo, you undastand wat Cabral saying?

JOJO: Yeah.

BEAR: Manny, you like I put my hands ova his ears so he no can hear?

MANNY: He not dat young.

BEAR: Okay, just checking. Go 'head, Cabral.

CABRAL: So da night befo' da fight, he go sleep wit' Ruby and give all his strength to her.

CHAMP: Aeh, Manny, not my fault. She too cute. I no can say no.

CABRAL: So I dunno wat fo' tell Sam, eh. I was supposed to watch Champ, and I no like lie to Sam.

CHAMP: You told Sam da truth. You said I wen' sleep early dat night. You just neva tell 'um I wen' sleep wit' one girl.

CABRAL: Sure enough, his legs give out in da second round. Round two! Flat on his ass.

(OLDER MANNY *sits down beside* MANNY.)

MANNY: Wat kine guy he was?

CABRAL: One haole from da army.

BEAR: No lie! Awww, shame, man, shame. You wash up, Champ, if one haole can wipe you out. Hang up your jocks, pau, finish already.

CHAMP: Shaddup. You dunno why I lost. You know why I lost?

BEAR: Yeah, da haole wen' knock you out.

CHAMP: Damn haole hit me one low blow. Supposed to be one foul.

BEAR: Yeah? If one foul, how come da ref neva call 'um?

CHAMP: Wise up, stupid, damn ref was one haole too. Favaratism, 's why I lost. Juice, man, juice.

MANNY: 'S why hard.

BEAR: 'S why hard wen you good fo' nuttin'.

CHAMP: Aeh, I was getting 'um good, man. Try come, try come here. I show you. (*CHAMP grabs BEAR around the head with one arm and with the other throws punches to BEAR's head.*) Manny, was li'dis. I was punching da guy out, see, boom, boom, boom, da ref was trying to break us up. So da guy like run away, so I did dis (*steps on BEAR's foot*) so he no can move and boom, boom—

(*BEAR gets away.*)

BEAR: No wonda you wen' lose. You not one boxer, you one dirty wrestler.

CHAMP: I see you like one boxing lesson. C'mon, I take you on. Go 'head, try someting.

(*CHAMP dances around BEAR, throwing jabs and punches.*)

BEAR: Aeh, aeh, arm wrestle, arm wrestle. You scared?

CHAMP: You no mo' chance against me. Give up already.

BEAR: Lemme see, lemme see! (*BEAR goes down on his belly, arm up and poised for action. CHAMP locks his hand into BEAR's.*) Aeh, Manny, you be da judge. No let dis bugga cheat.

CHAMP: Me? You da one going hit me one low blow.

MANNY: Okay, you guys, shaddup, shaddup. Get ready. (*MANNY sits on BEAR's back.*) Jojo, sit on Champ. Okay now, wen I say, "Go!"—

(*CHAMP quickly pins BEAR's arm down.*)

BEAR: Aeh, aeh, you see, you see! Da bugga cheating, I told you, man!

CHAMP: Wassamadda, he said, "Go."

MANNY: Not yet. Listen, wen I say, "Go," den you go. On your mark, get set—"Go!"

(*BEAR and CHAMP grunt and struggle against each other as JOJO, MANNY, OLDER MANNY, and CABRAL hoot and holler. It looks like BEAR is going to win, but CHAMP comes on strong and finally pins BEAR, who rolls on his back exhausted.*)

BEAR: Beer, beer. (*CABRAL pours beer from above onto BEAR's face.*) Aeh, no waste 'um li'dat! Gimme.

(*He sits up for his beer.*)

CHAMP: Manny, da bugga weak. I tought I was wrestling one girl.

BEAR: Wat you mean? Not my fault I get sore back. Aeh, I get Manny on my back, and you only get Jojo. No fair. Big weight diff'rence.

CHAMP: Excuses, always excuses.

BEAR: Aeh, I get sore back, no joke. I was lifting heavy boxes at work. You ask Manny.

MANNY: Aeh, wait. How should I know?

BEAR: Chee, Manny, I told you wat happen.

MANNY: Yeah but I dunno if dat was true.

CHAMP: Yeah, you dumb bastard.

BEAR: Aeh, no call me dumb. At least I no let one haole beat me.

CHAMP: I told you he wen' foul me.

BEAR: Excuses, always excuses.

CABRAL: Aeh, look at me. I ain't one no good haole. I one good Portogee.

(BEAR *puts an arm around* CABRAL'*s shoulders.*)

BEAR: 'S right, man. Manny, I love dis Portogee like he was my own bruddah. You no can find one betta Portogee dan dis guy. He give us Portogee sausage, Portogee sweet bread, malasadas—

CABRAL: Aeh, aeh.

BEAR: Wat?

CABRAL: I get someting you like o' wat?

BEAR: Aeh, wat kine guy you tink me? Chee, here I telling everybody you my buddy and you tink I looking fo' your money. Aeh, man, you make one puka, right here in my heart.

CABRAL: Okay, so you no like borrow money?

BEAR: No, no. I no like borrow nuttin'. But, you know, I get dese small flags I can sell you.

CABRAL: 'S wat I tought. No get too close, eh, brah.

BEAR: Aeh, man, dis one business deal. Da flags get fifty stars. I sell 'um to you fo' fifty cents each and you can sell 'um fo' one dollar each. Good souvenir fo' statehood.

CABRAL: Come kiss my ass. Bugga no can count to ten, but put one dollar sign in front of da numba and he can count to tousand.

(*Everybody has a good laugh. They settle down for more beer.*)

CHAMP: Damn hot, eh.

CABRAL: Hot and sticky.

(CABRAL *blows inside his shirt.* BEAR *fans himself with his hand.*)

MANNY: Aeh, Bear, tell da guys wat wen' happen at da beach.

CHAMP: Wat? You wen' naked and all da girls wen' faint?

BEAR: No get funny. Some service guys wen' get sassy wit' Gladys and Sheila.

CHAMP: Gladys and Sheila? Damn haoles go afta anyting.

BEAR: So dis one bugga wen' say, "Wanna hot dog, honey, you be da bun and I'll be da wienee."

CHAMP: 'S all? You act da same way wit' da haole wahines. In fact, you mo' dirty and sickening.

BEAR: I was going rap da haole in da face but two MPs wen' pass by. Jam everyting up. I was all set fo' one good fight and—

CHAMP: Yeah, yeah, I bet da haole could chop you down real easy.

BEAR: Look who talking.

CABRAL: See, da trouble is dese service guys come here, like make out wit' our wahines, eh. Den dey give da girls V.D. And whose hard luck? Us guys, man. 'Cause den we catch da disease from da girls.

JOJO: Get one good haole in my class. Real nice guy. We wen' elect him class president. Why you guys hate da haoles?

BEAR: Jojo, you no undastand. See, we no hate all da haoles. Sure, get good haoles too, but no ask me where dey stay 'cause I neva meet one yet.

CHAMP: Yeah, Manny, you no tell your bruddah nuttin' o' wat?

MANNY: Wat you like I tell 'um?

CABRAL: Tell 'um about da no-good haoles.

MANNY: Jojo, da haoles no good, no be friends wit' dem.

BEAR: Yeah, you listen to your bruddah.

JOJO: I tink haoles okay.

CABRAL: Manny, you get one hardhead bruddah.

CHAMP: Dey no good, Jojo, dey hit you below da belt.

BEAR: Dey like talk fancy, eh, use hybolic words, act like dey know everyting.

CABRAL: Dey like act bossy. Orda you around—do dis, do dat. And wat you tink dey doing? Sitting on deir fat asses watching you work your ass off. Dey let you do all da dirty work, jus' like my boss. Someday I going broke his mout'.

JOJO: But, Manny, if you going Mainland, you gotta mix wit' da haoles, eh? You gotta be friends wit' dem.

CHAMP: Aeh, wat dis about Mainland?

CABRAL: You neva say nuttin' about going to da Mainland.

MANNY: Nah, jus' talk, nuttin'.

BEAR: If you going Mainland, who I going hang around wit'? You no can go.

MANNY: Why? You like live in dis alley all your life?

BEAR: No. Someday I going get one place by da beach, maybe Waianae side.

CABRAL: Where you going get da money buy one place?

BEAR: 'S easy. Drive da tourists around da island, show 'um da sights, t'row 'um some bullshit. I know wat dey like see: Punchbowl, Crouching Lion, Chinaman Hat. I tell 'um stories about da menehunes. Dey going eat 'um up.

CHAMP: Maybe I betta give up boxing and go to Maui.

CABRAL: Give up boxing? You crazy? You going be da next middleweight champion of da world.

CHAMP: Yeah, yeah. But you know Ruby like I marry her and go back live wit' her parents. She like I go help wit' da family farm.

BEAR: You on one farm? Wat you going do, t'row cow shit all ova da ground?

CHAMP: Aeh, you dunno nuttin' o' wat? You no call 'um cow shit, you call 'um manure.

CABRAL: You no can give up your career fo' one wahine.

CHAMP: Ruby all right. She said da farm going be ours someday. 'S someting, eh. Betta dan nuttin'.

MANNY: Wat kine farm?

CHAMP: Dey raise onions.

BEAR and CABRAL: Onions?!

CHAMP: Yeah, onions, so wat?

CABRAL: But you hate onions, you no can stand onions. Every time we orda saimin, you gotta tell 'um no put onions inside.

BEAR: Yeah, I rememba da day dey put onions in anyway, and you wen' take each one out and mess up da table wit' onions. Make ass, man.

CHAMP: I no like eat onions, but I can grow 'um

CABRAL: I know you, you even smell one onion, you like t'row up.

BEAR: I can just see you t'rowing cow shit around fo' raise someting you hate eat.

CHAMP: Aeh, I neva said I going. I said maybe, so watch it.

OLDER MANNY: Aeh, Champ, no listen to dese guys. If you like go Maui, go. Betta live on Maui dan here in da alley. Betta live on one farm wit' fresh air dan in one rotten gym wit' stinking sweat in your nose all da time.

CABRAL: Yeah, you know wat? Dis place too damn small. You go here,

you go dere, you always run into somebody you know. No mo' fun
da kine, you no can do nuttin' sneaky. I tink I going join da Marines.

BEAR: Dey no like 4-F buggas like you.

CABRAL: Wat you mean, 4-F? *(He snaps to attention and salutes smartly.)*
General Cabral, six-star general.

CHAMP: 'S wat we need—one good war.

BEAR: Yeah, wit' you on da odda side.

CHAMP: You looking fo' it, eh, you really looking fo' it.

BEAR: Yeah, I looking fo' your brain, but I no see nuttin'.

(CHAMP shows BEAR a fist.)

CHAMP: You like see dis in your face?

MANNY: Aeh, you assholes, cool head, eh. Too damn hot now.

CHAMP: I like change da map of his face little bit.

BEAR: I make your face nuttin' but detours.

JOJO: Aeh, wait, I tink I hear somebody coming.

*(The gang hides in the shadows. JEANIE and SWEENEY enter. He's
dressed in a short-sleeved plaid shirt and khaki pants.)*

JEANIE: Well, you betta go now. I gotta get home.

SWEENEY: I thought maybe I'd take you to your front door.

JEANIE: No, I'm okay.

SWEENEY: Meeting you at the bowling alley was lucky for me. I was getting bored at the Y. Can I see you again?

JEANIE: I work at the alley, so if you like bowling . . .

SWEENEY: Some of my buddies went looking for dames, but I had my
eye out for somebody special. Someone like you.

JEANIE: Well, you know, I get one boyfriend.

SWEENEY: Yeah, I got a girl in Oregon. Her name's Margie. I kinda hope
she's waiting for me, but . . . Been to Oregon?

JEANIE: No, neva left da Islands.

SWEENEY: Oregon's got some nice beaches too. Different from Hawai'i's
but still beautiful. Maybe you'll visit me sometime.

JEANIE: Maybe. Well, gotta go.

SWEENEY: Wait. I was thinking maybe we could go have some coffee
and talk.

JEANIE: I don't think so. Too late.

SWEENEY: I got no place to go. Haven't talked to a pretty girl in I don't
know how long.

MANNY: Aeh, haole, wat you tink you doing here? *(The gang emerges and surrounds* SWEENEY.*)* You no going answer me? Who you tink you, eh?

JEANIE: Manny . . .

MANNY: Shaddup.

SWEENEY: I guess you two know each other. Sorry. I just met her tonight. I mean, hey, I wasn't trying anything.

BEAR: Lying bastard.

MANNY: You tink you was going get one easy time wit' her, eh?

JEANIE: Leave 'um alone. He neva do nuttin'. Let 'um go.

MANNY: Go 'way.

JEANIE: No.

MANNY: You like I kick your ass home?

SWEENEY: Boy, nobody told me the natives would be restless tonight.

CHAMP: Aeh, you making fun of us?

SWEENEY: No, don't take it the wrong way. I was just kidding.

CABRAL: We not laughing.

SWEENEY: Yeah, yeah. Hey, ah, wait. My friends call me Sweeney.

MANNY: We wen' ask you fo' your name? Wat da hell we care wat your name?

SWEENEY: Listen, I'm stationed at Pearl and—

CHAMP: One sailor boy, eh. I hear you guys get one girl in every port.

CABRAL: Yeah, you tink you one real lova, eh, one real Casanova.

SWEENEY: Bet I could learn a lot from you guys.

BEAR: Getting mo' and mo' cocky.

MANNY: You tink you so tarrific, eh, you really looking fo' trouble.

SWEENEY: No, no. Hey, why don't we shake and be friends, huh?

JOJO: I be your friend.

MANNY: Shaddup!

JOJO: We go be friends wit' him.

SWEENEY: Yeah, that's great, yeah.

*(*SWEENEY *offers his hand to* JOJO. MANNY *shoves* JOJO *aside.* OLDER MANNY *stands next to* MANNY.*)*

MANNY: I said go home now!

JEANIE: Manny, he was only lonesome to talk to somebody.

MANNY: 'S wat you tink.

CABRAL: How 'bout we teach dis haole one lesson?

CHAMP: He tink he hot shit.

> (SWEENEY *tries to get away, but* MANNY *blocks him.*)

MANNY: Where you tink you going, haole?

BEAR: You going get your medicine.

JOJO: Manny, no cause trouble.

MANNY: Go home befo' I slap your head. You hear me?

> (MANNY *shoves* JOJO, *who falls backward to the ground.*)

BEAR: Aeh, haole, we going make sure you neva come dis way again.

MANNY: I take my cut first.

> (MANNY *throws a couple of punches, then the rest of the gang piles into*
> SWEENEY, *punching and kicking until he crumples to the ground.*
> JEANIE *runs off.* OLDER MANNY *stands aside, watching solemnly.*)

BEAR: Weak bugga.

CABRAL: Wat you expect from one haole.

CHAMP: I got in one low blow fo' payback.

MANNY: Get your ass going. And if you like mo' trouble, you know
where you can find us.

> (SWEENEY *struggles to get up, then stumbles weakly out of the alley.*)

BEAR: Now I can sleep good tonight.

CABRAL: Yeah, I had my fun.

CHAMP: I see you guys, eh.

CABRAL: You going see Ruby?

CHAMP: Aeh, I get my fighting, now I going get my loving.

CABRAL: Ruby get somebody fo' me?

CHAMP: One hard-up bugga like you? No make me laugh.

CABRAL: Aeh, c'mon, wat about her friend, da one wit' da missing finga?

> (CHAMP *exits laughing, with* CABRAL *right behind.*)

BEAR: Manny, you like go eat someting?

MANNY: Nah.

BEAR: I feel like some won ton min.

> (BEAR *exits.*)

MANNY: I told you go home, why you neva listen?

JOJO: Da haole neva do nuttin' to you. Fo' wat beat him up?

MANNY: 'Cause I no like his looks. I no like haoles getting smart wit' me.

JOJO: He wanted to be friends.

MANNY: Aeh, no haole going take me cheap, undastand?

JOJO: Was four against one.

MANNY: So wat? If your haoles wen' trap me, you tink dey going give me chance? You tink dey care about me? Use your head, dammit, wat da hell you good fo' if you act dumb! Next time you listen wen I tell you someting.

JOJO: I no need listen to you, you not my faddah.

MANNY: Wat, wat you said? You talking back to me?

JOJO: You only act like him, good fo' nuttin, like Mama said.

MANNY: Wat kine shit she been telling you?

JOJO: And I no like da way you sponge off Mama.

MANNY: She said dat?

JOJO: She trying her best fo' us and wat you doing—

MANNY: Bullshit! She trying her best screw da bums around here.

JOJO: Wat you mean?

MANNY: Yeah, one greasy bastard! He putting his hands all ova her using her to get his kicks! You undastand me? She sleeping wit' da bum!

JOJO: Shaddup! No talk about Mama li'dat! Shaddup!

(JOJO lunges at MANNY, who pushes him off continuously, as JOJO is relentless.)

MANNY: And she love it, you hear me, she no can get enough of dat fucking punk. She like he touch her wit' his dirty hands, she like he kiss her wit' his pilau mout'! Wassamadda, you no can take da truth? You just one damn kid, you dunno shit!

(MANNY whacks JOJO across the back with his hand and hurls him to the ground.)

JOJO: I hate you! Wat you good fo'? I shame call you my bruddah, I no mo' bruddah!

(JOJO runs off.)

OLDER MANNY: Jojo, wait! Jojo! Manny, go afta him. Tell 'um you sorry. Tell 'um you was wrong. 'S all you gotta say. No let him tink dat about Mama. Go befo' too late. Manny! Manny! Do someting, you stupid shit! You fuck up your life, no do da same ting to Jojo.

(MANNY, silent and frustrated, stalks off in the opposite direction. Lights down. Lights up. It is now morning. JEANIE and MAMA enter.)

JEANIE: I told Manny come see you befo' we go to da airport but . . .

MAMA: Manny okay?

JEANIE: Yeah, but he no act dat happy about going to da Mainland.

MAMA: Where you folks going live?

JEANIE: Los Angeles. Going be okay. We had one good, long talk and he said he going change. He promise. We going get married in L.A. I get some money saved up. And we going stay wit' my sista and her husband first. No worry. I take care of Manny.

MAMA: Wat Manny going do on da Mainland?

JEANIE: My sista's husband get one service station. Manny can work dere till he find someting betta.

(OLDER MANNY *edges closer to* MAMA.)

MAMA: If Manny's faddah neva die, maybe we wen' move away from here long ago. He used to talk about going to da Mainland too, wen Manny was one kid. But den Jojo was born, so was too hard. If neva get Jojo, maybe Manny's life would be diff'rent. I dunno. Maybe. I betta go work.

JEANIE: Wait fo' Manny. He in da pool hall telling Uji goodbye. He said give dis to you. (*She hands the envelope to* MAMA, *who fingers it knowingly.*) I go inside get him.

OLDER MANNY: Wait, Mama, no go yet. I like see you.

(JEANIE *exits into the pool hall.* MAMA *looks into the envelope and quickly closes it.*)

OLDER MANNY: Mama, I returning da money to you. 'S yours. You need 'um. No go yet. I like talk to you. I like tell you . . . I like tell you . . . I was so young dat time. I neva tink about how hard was fo' you. Now I can see. You know wat I mean? Let me see your face, Mama. Try look dis way. (*She doesn't move.*) Wat you tinking, Mama? Tell me.

MANNY (*from inside pool hall*): Yeah, we going be okay. I going miss your saimin and laulau.

(MAMA *slowly starts to exit.*)

MAMA: Bye-bye, Manny. Take care yourself.

OLDER MANNY: Wait, Mama, no go. Wait! Waaaiii—

MANNY: Yeah, okay. T'anks.

(MAMA *is gone, as* MANNY, JEANIE, *and* UJI *appear from the pool hall.*)

UJI: Manny, if tings no work out on da Mainland, no shame come home. Going always get one place fo' you in Hawai'i.

(UJI *exits.*)

JEANIE: She gone already.

OLDER MANNY: Why you neva come out mo' quick? She was here. You stayed in da pool hall too long.

JEANIE: Go see her at da cafe. I know she like talk to you.

MANNY: You wen' give her da envelope? *(She nods.)* Why she neva wait fo' me?

JEANIE: She said she hadda go work.

OLDER MANNY: Tell her you sorry. Tell her you not going to da Mainland. Stay in Hawaiʻi and help her. Go school. Make Mama's life mo' easy. Do 'um befo' too late. And you gotta help Jojo do good. Wat he going do wit'out you?

MANNY: I no mo' nuttin' to say to her. Too late.

OLDER MANNY: Not too late. Listen to me, not too late. Hurry up, hurry up, go.

MANNY: I just like get away from here. I wish someday dey tear down dis place and cova 'um up wit' cement. I hate dis island. No mo' chance fo' guys like me. Da soona I get outta here, da betta. I neva coming back to Hawaiʻi.

OLDER MANNY: 'S wat you tink. You dunno wat you talking about. Go, run away, you lolo asshole. See wat you get. No come cry to me later and tink I going help. *(As MANNY and JEANIE exit, the lights dim to a soft spotlight on OLDER MANNY.)* So we went Mainland live. Was okay. Except afta four years, me and Jeanie wen' split up. Not her fault. I not da easiest guy to live wit'. I hear she married one jewelry salesman, and dey living in San Jose, California. No mo' kids, but at least da husband one good guy. I mean, I hope so. I dunno. Sometimes I tink I like visit Jeanie and tell her hi, long time no see. But wat good dat going do? I had my chance. You know, Bear driving one taxi now in Honolulu. I hear he doing okay. And Cabral, Marine Sergeant Walter M. Cabral, was killed in action at Con Thien, Vietnam. Champ living da good life as one gentleman farmer on Maui. Sitting pretty raising onions. My bruddah Jojo — Joseph — graduated from University of Hawaiʻi. At least my muddah wen' live to see dat. Yeah, Jojo get good head. He working as one accountant at Castle & Cooke. Married one local girl, get two kids, one boy and one girl. 'S wat I hear. I neva see him afta I left Hawaiʻi. Jojo did good wit'out me. Maybe good I wasn't around boddaring him. My muddah — she died about eight years afta I went to da Mainland. Brain hemorrhage o' someting. And I neva know 'cause I was traveling around da country looking fo' jobs—and good times. So I neva had chance talk to my muddah. To tell her I was sorry. I neva know she was going die so soon. Why I stayed in da pool hall so long wen she was waiting outside? You tink I was wrong give her back da envelope? But dat was her money. She need 'um. Why I neva go to da cafe talk to her? Nobody was stopping me but me. Wen you young, you get hard head, I guess. You tink you know all da answers. If only I can go back in time and fix tings up. Wen I heard my muddah died, I wen' crazy tinking I like just one wish, 's all I ask. I prayed real hard, all my might. Let me go back to 1959, let me live ova dat part of my life so I can change all da bad tings, so I can do da right tings fo' my muddah. But I neva get one magic lamp so . . . Aeh, I gotta go. Busy, you know. Singing Hawaiian songs wit' dis troupe I play wit' on da Mainland. Singing about Hawai'i, da beauty of da Islands, da happy people of paradise —all da time knowing dat da only way I going back to Hawai'i fo' good is wen I ma-ke, die, dead. And not befo' dat. 'S why hard. *(Spotlight fades slowly to black as* OLDER MANNY *closes the play, singing one stanza of Kui Lee's song, "Days of Our Youth.")*

THE END

A'ala Park, Kumu Kahua Theatre, 1997, directed by James A. Nakamoto.
Iwalani Campman as Jeanie and Warren Fabro as Young Manny.
PHOTO BY COREY LUM.

A'ala Park, Kumu Kahua Theatre, 1997, directed by James A. Nakamoto. Jojo (Kawika Allen) gives the birthday cake to his mother (Laura Baring). PHOTO BY COREY LUM.

A'ala Park, Kumu Kahua Theatre, 1997, directed by James A. Nakamoto. Warren Fabro *(left)* as Young Manny and Ray Bumatai as Older Manny. PHOTO BY COREY LUM.

A'ala Park, Kumu Kahua Theatre, 1997, directed by James A.
Nakamoto. Cabral (Daryl Bonilla, *right*) gives sparring pointers to
Champ (Michael Ng). PHOTO BY COREY LUM.

A'ala Park, Kumu Kahua Theatre, 1997, directed by James A.
Nakamoto. Uji-san (Larry Fukumoto, *left*) asks Bear (Jarod Bailon) to
get rid of a dead cat he found by the pool hall. PHOTO BY COREY LUM.

Stew Rice

Cast of Characters

RUSSELL SHIMA

BENJAMIN LEE

ROLAND "ZIPPY" CHING

RUBY OGAWA

SHARON UCHIDA

DONNA WONG

TIME: Act 1, 1957–1958; Act 2, 1978

PLACE: Various spots on Oahu

SCENERY: A simple set sparsely decorated. Cubes of various sizes on stage. Upstage area may be decorated with Hawaiian scenes of past years. A couch is used in Act 2.

Act One

Scene 1

(*RUSSELL SHIMA enters and addresses the audience.*)

SHIMA: Hi. Welcome to Hawai'i 1957. Well, you gotta use your imagination. This is the Hawai'i before statehood. When rock and roll was king but Alfred Apaka was still popular singing songs of Old Hawai'i. When the Royal Hawaiian and the Moana were the best hotels in Waikiki. My name is Russell Shima. Shima in Japanese means "island." Some people on the Mainland like to ask if my name translates into anything. Sometimes I say it means "Turtle rising out of the sea without its shell." They love it.

(*ZIPPY CHING and BENJAMIN LEE enter and sit on cubes.*)

This is a play about my two buddies—Zippy Ching and Benjamin Lee—and me. Life is good in 1957 when we're juniors in high school, an all-boys' school. The best kind. Simple and uncomplicated. Come on, let's go. Back to that nostalgic time. Silly, happy, and full of memories.

(*SHIMA joins his friends.*)

Aeh, da dance hall look pretty good, man.

ZIPPY: Sure, wit' all da work we put in. How come I hadda help?

SHIMA: 'Cause I was da decoration chairman. 'S wat happen wen you my friend.

ZIPPY: Who said I was your friend?

LEE: Making da stars was real humbug.

ZIPPY: Nah, we only stayed up till t'ree dis morning making 'um.

SHIMA: Okay, okay, you guys, t'anks for helping wit' da decoration.

LEE: No sweat, no sweat.

ZIPPY: Aeh, t'anks for asking us.

LEE: Yeah, you wen' teach us one good lesson.

(ZIPPY and LEE nod at each other knowingly.)

SHIMA: Going be wort' it. Da girls going feel real romantic seeing dis place.

ZIPPY: Aeh, Ben, I like see your kiss-on-the-neck technique.

LEE: Okay, you can get front-row seat. See, you gotta hold 'um certain way, up close, like dis. Den you put your mout' right up to her ear— and you stick your tongue in.

ZIPPY: Aeh, no bull lie.

LEE: 'S da way to get da girls hot, I tell you.

SHIMA: How you know?

LEE: I read 'um in one magazine.

ZIPPY: Wat magazine?

LEE: *Sexology.*

SHIMA: How you wen' get hold of da magazine, you unda age?

LEE: Come on, Russ, you know I planning to go med school. Gotta do some advanced studies, read up on sex and all da kine stuff. Aeh, Zip, I going give you one tip. Wen dey announce da last dance tonight, take off one star and give 'um to da girl.

ZIPPY: Make ass, man.

LEE: Why? Dey like da kine romantic stuff. Den she can take home one souvenir and put 'um on her wall and dream about da tarrific guy who wen' send chills up her back and give her da fever.

ZIPPY: Yeah, den she find out all she had was da Hong Kong flu.

SHIMA: Girls sentimental, Zip. Dey like someting to rememba da best dance of deir lives.

ZIPPY: Our dance?

SHIMA: Of course. Da first dance of our junior year. Dis dance going set da standard for all da dances to come.

ZIPPY: Aeh, you tink da girls going laugh if dey find out I cannot dance?

SHIMA: Nah, no worry. Girls not like dat. Dey kindhearted.

LEE: Yeah, dey not going laugh in your face. Dey going laugh behind your back.

ZIPPY: 'S it, man, I ain't coming.

SHIMA: You see? 'S wat happen wen you neva come to da dances last year.

ZIPPY: Aeh, no rub 'um in, eh. Not my fault I was playing cowboys and Indians in my sophomore year. I had one long childhood. (*LEE takes off his T-shirt and throws it in* ZIPPY'S *face.*) Aeh, aeh, da stink, man. Make sure you bafe tonight, eh. I no like da girls faint from lack of oxygen. Phew!

(ZIPPY *throws the T-shirt high in the air and* LEE *catches it.*)

SHIMA: So you coming tonight, right?

ZIPPY: I coming but I not going dance.

LEE: Why?

ZIPPY: I told you. I dunno how dance.

LEE: You know. You wen' learn in da nint' grade like us.

ZIPPY: I forget already.

SHIMA: Dance da slow ones. All you gotta do is go side to side. You know. (SHIMA *demonstrates.*)

LEE: Yeah, and feel da wahines up.

ZIPPY: Dat I can do.

LEE: Tonight try dis. Wen you dancing wit' da girl, get your right leg moving between her legs.

ZIPPY: Come on!

LEE: Yeah, and make sure her right leg going between your legs.

ZIPPY: No!

LEE: Yeah, man, get you hot.

ZIPPY: Da girl not going get piss off?

LEE: No, she like get hot too. See, you hold her real close (*demonstrates*) and rock side to side. And sometimes forward and back. And make sure you slip your leg in just da right time. See? See my right leg? In, and brush her right leg. Man, she going be so hot.

SHIMA: Yeah, and no forget give her one balloon too.

ZIPPY: One star and one balloon? How she going dance?

SHIMA: Esalay, brah. She hold da balloon in her right hand, da star in her left, and she put bot' arms around your neck.

LEE: Dat way, wen you bring your hands down to her okole, she no can do nuttin'.

ZIPPY: You crazy.

LEE: Well, 's up to you. 'S wat I going do.

SHIMA: Zip, dese girls fast. Seniors.

ZIPPY: Yeah, how come we wen' invite seniors?

LEE: Kaneko heard dey was fast.

ZIPPY: I no trust Kaneko.

SHIMA: Olda women betta anyway.

ZIPPY: But wat if dey tink we just kids?

LEE: Das why, no make ass.

SHIMA: And no step on deir feet wen you dance. And no tell 'um you cannot dance da fast ones, and—

ZIPPY: But I dunno how dance fast.

LEE: No guts, Ching, 's you, no guts.

ZIPPY: I dunno how do da bop. No kidding, I not lying.

LEE: Just rememba, no make ass.

ZIPPY: If I tell da girl I dunno how dance fast, I going make ass. If I try dance fast, I going make ass. Wat I going do?

SHIMA and LEE: Make ass!!

 (ZIPPY *tries to exit but* LEE *stops him.*)

LEE: You going enjoy yourself tonight even if we gotta drag you on da dance floor.

SHIMA: Aeh, no mo' time already. Gotta finish cleaning up da place.

LEE: Who making da food?

ZIPPY: Nagatani.

LEE: I ain't eating. Da bugga no wash his hands for nuttin'.

ZIPPY: He not making da food himself. His muddah and sistas going make everyting.

LEE: You sure?

SHIMA: 'S why dey pick Nagatani. He get four sistas can help.

 (*They exit.*)

Scene 2

 (*The song "Party Doll" by Buddy Knox begins.* RUBY, DONNA, *and* SHARON *enter from different directions in casual clothes. They work on their toenails, fingernails, makeup.*)

SHARON: Aeh, how come we wen' accept one dance wit' juniors?

DONNA: Yeah, dey going be uji.

RUBY: No can help. Actually was one mistake. Janet tought was anodda club and dat dey were seniors like us. Wen we found out, was too late to take da invitation back.

SHARON: Really embarrassing. Wat if people find out . . .

DONNA: Cradle robbas!

SHARON: Gaawwdd, and from one all-boys' school yet. Dey da worse, man.

DONNA: Da kine guys neva know how dance.

RUBY: 'S true. Especially da fast ones.

DONNA: All dey like do is dance close and feel you up.

SHARON: Wat wrong wit' dat?

DONNA: Sharon!

SHARON: Well, 's wat all da guys like do. Young or old.

RUBY: Yeah, Donna. I bet even your faddah feel up your muddah in deir bedroom.

DONNA: Aeh, no talk dirty.

SHARON: You know once I wen' open my folks' bedroom door and I wen' catch dem fooling around.

DONNA: Dey was naked?

SHARON: No, but dey was fooling around, you know.

DONNA: I dunno.

SHARON: You know, no act so dumb.

DONNA: I dunno nuttin'. All I know is wat you tell me.

SHARON: Well, use your imagination.

(DONNA tries to imagine.)

RUBY: Anyway, da guys tonight only one year younga dan us. Not going be dat bad.

SHARON: Dey going be uji, but 's okay. We can pay for our sins one night out of da year by being good girls.

DONNA: Sharon, wat kind position your muddah and faddah was in?

SHARON: Wat?

DONNA: I trying to imagine dem making love but kinna hard.

SHARON: Donna, I neva mean literally. Gawd, how embarrassing to tink you was imagining my folks making love.

DONNA: I know. Da next time I see dem, I cannot look dem in da face.

RUBY: You two getting good fun or wat?

DONNA: I kinna worried about tonight. Wat if da guys try grab ass? I going hit 'um.

SHARON: Dey can grab my ass.

DONNA: Sharon!

SHARON: But 's all.

DONNA: Dey betta not try kiss me.

SHARON: Dey can kiss me.

DONNA: Sharon!

SHARON: But dey betta not French-kiss me.

RUBY: Look, we not going marry dem.

DONNA: Maybe we betta not go.

SHARON: You betta not go. I going.

RUBY: Dis is just one dance. A small, little, innocent dance wit' junior boys who will act like gentlemen da whole night and nuttin' will happen.

SHARON: How boring. Ruby, you no mo' romantic spirit, yeah?

RUBY: I no mo' time tink about romance. I get lotta tings I like do and I no like get tied down wit' one lazy, cheating husband and bratty kids.

DONNA: You so clear-headed, I get jealous sometimes.

RUBY: I know wat I want. And it's not in Hawai'i. I wanna travel all ova da world and meet all kinds of men. I don't want to be stuck wit' a small-minded guy in Hawai'i who like drink beer wit' his friends and go to football games on Saturday.

DONNA: You know, Ruby, you so mature for your age.

SHARON: And so depressing. You wen' jus' describe my faddah.

RUBY: I wasn't talking about your faddah. I was talking about Hawai'i guys in general.

DONNA: Yeah, Sharon, no take it so personal. Sound like she was talking about my bruddah, Beer Belly Bobby.

RUBY: So anyway, tonight is only a tiny fraction of our lives, and we going donate it as our good deed for 1957.

DONNA: Good deed? Da vestal virgins go to da sacrificial altar.

SHARON: Wat if you not one virgin?

DONNA: You not one virgin?

SHARON: Of course . . . I one virgin. But I was almost not one virgin.

DONNA: Wat you did? Neva mind, no tell me. I make up for you. I neva even let one boy kiss me yet.

SHARON: No lie. You frigid or wat?

DONNA: Yeah, frigid like one Popsicle. If one boy try kiss me, his mout' going stuck to my face.

(The girls laugh and exit.)

Scene 3

(SHIMA enters dressed for the dance. Sonny James' "Young Love" begins. SHIMA practices dance steps. ZIPPY enters.)

SHIMA: Aeh, Zip, you wearing sharkskin pants, eh? Looking good.

ZIPPY: Wat about you, gabardine? Expensive, eh?

SHIMA: Nah, Sears Roebuck.

(LEE enters, wearing a long-sleeved pink shirt with cufflinks and gray slacks.)

LEE: Aeh, Russ, check me out, man. How I look?

SHIMA: Shaka, brah, shaka.

ZIPPY: You get guts wear pink shirt, man.

LEE: Wat? You dunno nuttin'? Pink is da color of da season. Check da pants, man, check 'um out. Gray sharkskin trousers. Pink and gray, da numba one color combination of our generation. McInerny's.

ZIPPY: Chee, Ben, you went all out, yeah.

SHIMA: Ben, you going put da girls to shame. Dey cannot look as good as you.

LEE: See da French cuffs and da cufflinks? My shoes, put your baby brown eyes on my shoes.

ZIPPY: Suede?

LEE: Correct. Suede. Genuine suede.

(ZIPPY and SHIMA go down on their knees to examine the shoes.)

ZIPPY: Man, real nice. Russ, try feel dis.

(The three girls enter in party dresses, full of crinolines.)

SHARON: Try look. Dose guys on the floor kissing da odda guy's feet.

RUBY: Dey not kissing his feet.

DONNA: Dey sure must like shoes.

SHARON: Or dey really nearsighted.

LEE: Aeh, da girls came, da girls came.

ZIPPY: Where?

SHIMA: Ova dere.

(SHIMA *and* ZIPPY *scramble to their feet.*)

ZIPPY: Wat dey look like?

LEE: Look out, you guys, shaddup, shaddup, no make ass.

ZIPPY: Dey no look dat old.

LEE: I told you. Check 'um out, man, check 'um out.

SHIMA: Da one on da left kinna cute.

LEE: Oh, man, da right one really bitchin.

ZIPPY: Aeh, da music not kinna fast?

SHIMA: Wat you like, funeral music or wat? Go 'head go. Take your pick.

LEE: Zip, go dance wit' da one on da right. Tell me wat she like.

ZIPPY: Me? Wassamatta wit' you?

LEE: I no like dance da first dance.

SHIMA: Aeh, Ben, come on, you and me go.

LEE: Wat, you like go now?

SHIMA: Yeah, we go, wat da hell.

LEE: Yeah, yeah, we go, we go. You go, I follow.

SHIMA: No, you go, I follow.

LEE: Okay wait, we go togedda. Step for step.

SHIMA: You sure? Step for step?

LEE: Yeah, yeah, yeah. You ready? I ready, get ready.

SHIMA: Left foot first.

LEE: Left, right.

SHIMA: Wat?

LEE: Left go first, right?

SHIMA: Right, left.

LEE: Wait, wait. Which is right, right or left?

SHIMA: Left foot! Left foot! One, two, t'ree, go!

(SHIMA *and* LEE *both step out with the right foot, eyeing each other. They take several steps as if on a tightrope.* SHIMA *stops,* LEE *stops.* SHIMA *steps out again, so does* LEE. *They are halfway to the girls when the song ends. They freeze, look around sheepishly, then turn and walk back quickly.*)

LEE: Make ass, man, make ass.

ZIPPY: Wat you guys was doing?

LEE: Why you stop for?

SHIMA: 'Cause da music wen' stop.

LEE: You always li'dat, you know, Shima, you always li'dat.

SHIMA *(overlap)*: Shit, man, no blame me.

LEE: Aeh, I was all set to do my right-leg-in technique.

ZIPPY: I tought you saving dat for da last dance?

LEE: Nah, I ready already. *("You Send Me" by Sam Cooke plays.)* Go, man, go. Go, go, go. Go, Zippy, go.

ZIPPY: Wat?

LEE: Aeh, back me up, back me up.

ZIPPY: Me? How?

LEE: Ask one girl to dance. And no pull one Shima on me.

ZIPPY: I no like. Da t'ird record going be one fast one.

LEE: No, I talk to Kaneko tonight. He said da first set all t'ree songs going be slow.

ZIPPY: You sure?

LEE: 'S wat he said. So nobody hold back, like you. Now come on, before dis song finish. We go, we go. *(LEE and ZIPPY move toward the girls. LEE has his eye on RUBY. He looks back and sees ZIPPY wandering off, looking very innocent. LEE looks to SHIMA for encouragement. SHIMA motions him forward. LEE crosses to the girls, still looking at SHIMA. RUBY moves away from her spot a few seconds before LEE turns to ask for a dance.)* May I have . . . *(LEE is face to face with DONNA instead and is almost in shock. He recovers and shifts over to RUBY.)* May I have this dance?

RUBY: Sure.

(They go center stage to dance. ZIPPY timidly edges over to SHARON.)

ZIPPY: May I dance? *(He realizes his mistake and is embarrassed.)* I mean, no, ah, I can dance? No, no . . .

SHARON: Hi, you like dance? I do, t'ank you.

(SHARON leads ZIPPY to the dance floor.)

RUBY: How come most of da guys not dancing?

(LEE manages to sneak his right leg in between RUBY's legs. Then he tries dancing with her in that awkward position.)

LEE: Oh, I dunno, you know.

(Suddenly LEE grabs his right leg.)

RUBY: Wat happen?

LEE: I dunno. Ah, excuse, eh. I betta go. T'anks. My leg, aaahhh.

(SHIMA helps LEE limp back.)

SHIMA: Wassamatta?

LEE: I get one cramp, one cramp.

SHIMA: You bugga, your leg got all tensed up wen you wen' try your leg-in technique, right?

LEE: Da leg got in dere, man, da leg got in dere.

(The music ends. Then Bill Haley's "Rock Around the Clock" begins.)

ZIPPY: Kaneko!

(Offstage we hear KANEKO's hyena-like laugh. SHIMA pulls LEE with him to dance with DONNA and RUBY. LEE shakes off his cramp and does his best.)

SHARON: Oh, good song.

ZIPPY: Ah, ah, you know wat. I like dance da fast ones, but I gotta go because I tink I going t'row up.

SHARON: You one real joka, eh, you. Come on.

(She forces ZIPPY to dance. He is all arms and legs, awkwardly stepping on SHARON's right foot, then kicking her left shin. SHARON bends over in pain clutching her shin as ZIPPY accidentally knees her in the buttocks, sending her sprawling on the floor. Horrified, ZIPPY tries to help her up. SHARON rises, turns with her fists up in a boxing stance. ZIPPY raises his arms in surrender. There is a blackout, then time for the Last Dance. Johnny Mercer's "Dream" with the Four Aces begins. Dim lights go up.)

KANEKO *(offstage)*: Last dance, you guys! Last dance! *(hyena laugh)*.

(LEE comes out first, followed by SHIMA and ZIPPY. They grab stars and balloons and give them to their dance partners, RUBY, DONNA, and SHARON, respectively. They dance. As the song ends, the lights go down. All exit.)

Scene 4

(Buddy Holly's "Ready Teddy" plays. The boys run onstage, ready for school. The school bell rings and the boys scramble to their cube seats. Class starts.)

LEE: Wat? But Miss Gray, how come I gotta go first? My name is Lee, right? Asato should go first if you follow da alphabet. Oh, okay. *(Clears throat and stands.)* Dis is "Sir Galahad" by Lord Tennyson. "My good blade carves da casques of men." You know, Miss Gray, how come Tennyson neva say *helmets* instead of casques, so more clear? I had to look up *casques* in da dictionary. I woulda used *helmets of men.* . . . Oh, okay. "My tough lance t'rustet sure" . . . 'S one hard one. T'rustet. He shoulda said "my tough lance can poke da body." . . . Oh, okay. "My strengt' is da strengt' of ten, because my heart is pure." . . . Now I tink dat . . . Oh, okay.

(LEE *sits down triumphant.* SHIMA *rises;* LEE *mugs with* ZIPPY *as* SHIMA *reads dramatically with grand gestures.*)

SHIMA: The shattering trumpet shrilleth high, the hard brands shiver on the steel, the splinter'd spear-shafts rack and fly, the horse and rider reel, they reel they roll in clanging lists, and when the tide of combat stands, perfume and flowers fall in showers, that lightly rain from ladies hands. How sweet are looks that ladies bend on whom their favors fall! For them I battle till the end, to save from shame and thrall.

(School bell rings.)

LEE: Aeh, Russ, how you do dat?

SHIMA: Wat?

LEE: Talk like one haole. 'S good.

ZIPPY: Yeah, man, I close my eyes and I tought was one haole talking. Spooky, man.

SHIMA: You guys can talk good English in class wen you have to.

LEE: Yeah, I can talk good English, but I no sound like one haole. You sound like one haole. How you turn 'um off and on li'dat?

SHIMA: I dunno. I just can, 's all. I just can.

LEE: If I get accepted into Harvard, I gotta talk like one haole too.

SHIMA: I hope I get into Antioch.

LEE: Antioch College, no sweat. But I dunno why you like Antioch. Just because Miss Gray went dere?

SHIMA: No, not dat. I tinking of UCLA too or University of Washington, I dunno.

ZIPPY: Me, I like University of Oregon or Colorado State. I tired stay in Hawai'i. Gotta see wat on da odda side of da ocean.

LEE: You, too, Zip, gotta brush up on your English pronunciation. You no like talk pidgin English all your life.

ZIPPY: I know.

LEE: I no like you get embarrassed if da haoles laugh at you on da Mainland. You know how you sound.

ZIPPY: I no sound dat bad.

LEE: 'S wat you tink. Rough, man.

ZIPPY: You just as bad.

LEE: Aeh, I neva said I talk like one haole. You no hear me? I said I gotta learn how talk like one haole. And I pity da haoles if dey give me bad time.

SHIMA: Da scary part is we going be leaving home for da first time.

ZIPPY: I hope da haoles treat us betta dan we treat dem here.

SHIMA *(haolefied)*: Roland Zippy Ching, follow the Golden Rule and you will be rewarded with the fellowship of good haole friends who will treat you like the prince you are.

LEE: You damn haole, I gotta talk li'dat before I go to Harvard.

SHIMA: If you get accepted, you lolo limu.

ZIPPY: You know wat? If we all go different Mainland schools, we not going stay togedda anymo'.

LEE: I like da way you tink, Zippy, just like Einstein.

ZIPPY: But we been togedda since da t'ird grade.

SHIMA: You know da saying: all good tings must come to an end.

ZIPPY: Who said dat?

SHIMA: I dunno. Somebody famous, I guess. Maybe Shakespeare.

ZIPPY: But why we gotta separate?

LEE: Wat, you like we all go to University of Hawai'i?

ZIPPY: Not me. I gotta go to da Mainland.

SHIMA: Well den, see. 'S life. Wen boys become men, we walk different paths to manhood. Gotta be dat way.

ZIPPY: Sad, yeah.

SHIMA: I wonda wat life going be like wit'out you guys.

LEE: We going make new friends, 's all.

ZIPPY: But no can be as close as us guys now. 'S right, eh? Even if you make new friends, dey not going as close as us guys. I bet you.

SHIMA: No, you win. Not going be as good friends as us.

LEE: We still get one mo' year togedda. Den Harvard, Princeton, Stanford. My destiny awaits.

(He marches out with ZIPPY and SHIMA.)

Scene 5

(RUBY and SHARON enter in modest bathing suits, carrying beach towels.)

RUBY: Come on, Donna. You look silly like dat.

SHARON: Yeah, Donna, hurry up. Bumbai dey tink someting wrong wit' you.

(DONNA enters, wearing a sleeveless white blouse and walking shorts, but she also has a large towel on her head, hiding her face.)

RUBY: If you dat shame, why you wen' come for?

DONNA: 'S Sharon's fault.

SHARON: Me? Wat I did?

DONNA: You da one wen' accept one date wit' Roland.

SHARON: He wen' ask me so I said okay.

DONNA: But you neva have to include Ruby and me.

SHARON: Well, he said his friends like come too, so he ask me to ask you too.

RUBY: No blame Sharon, you didn't have to come.

SHARON: Yeah. You was curious. You sorta like Russell, I know.

(SHARON tugs at DONNA's towel.)

DONNA: No, no, no, no.

(DONNA scurries away and sits on a platform.)

RUBY: Donna, take off da towel.

DONNA: No.

SHARON: Please.

DONNA: I said no.

RUBY: I give up.

(SHARON and RUBY put their towels on the ground and sit to soak up the sun. SHIMA, LEE, and ZIPPY enter, holding paper cups of soda pop. They're wearing swimming trunks and T-shirts.)

LEE: Wassamadda wit' Donna?

SHIMA: Why you ask me?

LEE: She your date.

SHIMA: She not my date. Ask Zip.

ZIPPY: She not my date. Sharon my date.

SHIMA: You wen' arrange all dis, right?

ZIPPY: Not me, not me. Was Sharon. Her idea.

LEE: No lie.

ZIPPY: Honest. Aeh, you know I no mo' guts call her up. She wen' call me.

SHIMA: How she got your numba?

ZIPPY: She look 'um up in da phone book.

LEE: You kidding? Get one million Chings listed.

ZIPPY: Yeah? How many Chings living on Kohalamaunakea Drive?

SHIMA: You gave her your address?

ZIPPY: Well, I neva say 1526 Kohalamaunakea Drive. I just said, you know, we was just talking. And she said she live in Pauoa, and she ask me where I live, so, you know, I gotta answer and—

LEE: Okay, okay, neva mind. Back to my original question. Why Donna wearing da towel on her head?

SHIMA: She probably embarrassed to be wit' us.

ZIPPY: No, no, not dat. Okay, well, I guess I betta tell you. Sharon said no tell nobody, but okay—she shame of her pimples.

LEE: She get pimples? I neva notice.

SHIMA: She no mo' pimples. Her complexion good.

ZIPPY: 'S wat you tink, but she get plenny pimples, man. You just no can see 'um 'cause she put Clearasil on her face like Russ. Aeh, Clearasil is good for pimples, right?

SHIMA: I no see Clearasil on her face.

ZIPPY: How you can tell wit' da towel covering her face? Anyway, she using Clearasil like makeup, so she shame. Just no look too hard at her face.

(They proceed to the girls.)

SHARON: I hungry.

RUBY: Me too.

DONNA: Not me.

(The boys give the sodas to their girlfriends.)

LEE: Hope everybody like Pepsi.

RUBY: Oh yeah, t'anks.

ZIPPY: You like eat someting now?

SHARON: Well, Ruby and I tinking about getting hot dogs or someting.

ZIPPY: Okay, our treat, you know.

RUBY: No, no need do dat.

LEE: 'S okay, we brought money. We like treat you.

ZIPPY: We go.

SHARON: Oh, Donna not hungry yet.

LEE: Russ not hungry too.

SHIMA: Huh?

LEE: He can stay wit' her.

ZIPPY *(aside to* SHIMA*)*: No look at her face.

> *(*SHIMA *and* DONNA *are left alone as the others go off. There is an uncomfortable silence as* SHIMA *wanders around and tries to sneak a peek at* DONNA. *She clears her throat.)*

SHIMA: Wat?

DONNA: Huh?

SHIMA: You said someting?

DONNA: No.

SHIMA: Oh.

> *(There is silence again, but this time* DONNA *catches* SHIMA *looking at her.)*

DONNA: Why you staring at me?

SHIMA: Aaaaaahhhhh . . .

DONNA: Someting on my nose? I know not dat 'cause I already checked. Pimple on my forehead? I don't have pimples so not dat.

SHIMA: You sure?

DONNA: Wat?

SHIMA: I mean, no need be shame if you get pimples. See, I get some too. I use Clearasil like you.

DONNA: I don't use Clearasil. Wat for?

SHIMA: You no mo' pimples?

DONNA: Pimples? No. Why, my face look dat bad?

SHIMA: Oh no, your face is good. My face is bad. I mean, I get da pimples.

DONNA: I neva had problems wit' pimples, I dunno why but—

SHIMA: Oh, you lucky. I get oily skin so I put da stuff on, you know, wat I said.

DONNA: Oh.

SHIMA: I tought you put da towel on your head because you were embarrassed about pimples, but you no mo' pimples, so . . . why you get da towel like dat?

DONNA: Oh, dat, aaahhh, well, you know, da, da, da sun too hot for me. Sometimes I get sunburn so I gotta cova up.

SHIMA: Yeah, yeah. I get sunburn all da time, and da skin peel like crazy. Look real ugly, yeah. You know wen I peel da skin on my back, feels kinna good.

DONNA: Feels good?

SHIMA: Yeah, you know, you gotta get rid of da old wrinkled skin, yeah, so wen I peel da skin, I try see how big a piece I can peel off.

DONNA: And wat you do wit' da skin?

SHIMA: I put 'um all in one pile, den roll 'um togedda into one ball.

DONNA: Yeah? Den wat?

SHIMA: I eat 'um.

DONNA: Aaaauuuhhhhh.

SHIMA: Just kidding.

DONNA: You sure?

SHIMA: Yeah, I no eat 'um. I t'row 'um to my dog and he eat 'um.

DONNA: Aeeeehhh.

(There is a pause.)

SHIMA: Da guys taking long time, yeah.

(DONNA takes the towel off her head.)

DONNA: Ah, da dance last month was nice.

SHIMA: Da dance? Our club dance? It was okay, but nuttin' special.

DONNA: Oh, I guess you didn't like our club.

SHIMA: No, I neva mean dat. You girls were really nice. Sorry I stepped on your foot dat night.

DONNA: I didn't feel it.

SHIMA: I cannot dance dat good.

DONNA: I tought you really danced well. And, ah, I—

(There is laughter offstage. DONNA puts the towel back on her head. SHIMA moves away quickly.)

ZIPPY: How you like da plate lunch?

LEE: Da stew rice is okay, but my muddah's stew mo' ono.

ZIPPY: My muddah make really ono oxtail stew.

SHARON: Oxtail? You eat da tail of one ox?

ZIPPY: Get plenny meat on 'um.

LEE: Russ, your muddah know how make stew rice?

SHIMA: Of course, da best stew rice I eva ate.

LEE: You neva eat my muddah's beef stew.

SHIMA: Yeah, I did. Taste like Dinty Moore's.

LEE: Dinty Moore? Come on, man, Dinty Moore? You crazy.

SHIMA: Aeh, aeh, remember last year before da game wit' Kaimuki, was raining and we ate lunch at your house first?

LEE: Yeah, so wat?

SHIMA: And your muddah wen' feed us beef stew.

LEE: Yeah.

SHIMA: Well, da stew tasted like Dinty Moore.

LEE: You know why, eh, you know why?

SHIMA: No, why?

LEE: 'Cause dat time was Dinty Moore. My muddah wen' open couple a cans last minute just to feed us. But you neva eat my muddah's real stew.

ZIPPY: Russ, try look all da meat in dis stew rice. Ono, man.

SHIMA: Yeah, yeah. Aeh, wait. Wat dat?

ZIPPY: 'S meat, I told you. Get plenny meat.

SHIMA: No, no, look good. Wat kine meat get feelas and legs?

LEE: Wat? Aeh, aeh, 's one—

SHIMA: Cacaroach. You get one cacaroach in your stew.

SHARON: 'S one roach, all right. Big one too.

ZIPPY: I tink I going t'row up.

LEE: Aeh, wait, get your money back. Show da lunch wagon da caca-roach. You get one free lunch.

(ZIPPY exits.)

SHIMA: You know, if had one cacaroach, maybe had two or t'ree, maybe had one whole family, and you wen' eat da mama roach wit'out knowing.

LEE: Aeh, wen I was eating one piece, I felt like someting was tickling my t'roat wen I wen' swallow.

SHIMA: Musta been da little legs struggling against your t'roat. So da buggah was still alive.

(LEE hands his plate to SHIMA, then lies on the ground, moaning and groaning.)

RUBY: Wassamadda?

(RUBY kneels beside LEE, who immediately puts his head on her lap.)

RUBY: Not dat bad. People in some countries actually eat cockroaches.

SHIMA: He studying to be one doctor, but he kinna squeamish about certain tings.

(LEE turns his head and buries his face in RUBY's crotch area. She screams and hits him. Blackout.)

Scene 6

(Lights come up halfway on empty set, like it is dawn. The voice of a white radio disc jockey greets the radio audience.)

DISC JOCKEY: Ah, the sun's rising on Honolulu, and everything's right at K-P-O-I. Today, go ride the surf at Sunset Beach, pick seaweed at Ewa Beach, and be nice to tourists at Waikiki Beach. And you guys just returning from the submarine races at Hanauma Bay, tell me, tell me, who won? Call me, will ya? Okay, right here, right now, a special dedication to the guys and gals who'll be graduating this year. To the Class of 1958, here's the Everly Brothers singing their big hit, "All I Have to Do Is Dream."

(As the song plays, lights come up full. ZIPPY enters, carrying a bucket as the song fades away.)

ZIPPY: Aeh, you guys, come on. Hurry up! Da crabs no can wait!

(LEE and SHIMA carry in imaginary crab nets.)

LEE: Dis betta be good, Zip, dis betta be real good or I going tell your muddah we wen' buy *Sexology* magazine yesterday.

SHIMA: Ah, dis is da life.

ZIPPY: Da life of seniors.

LEE: Den college. Harvard, here I come.

ZIPPY: Aeh, Russ, try look da aku heads.

(They look in the bucket.)

SHIMA: Nice and bloody.

LEE: You sure get crabs here?

ZIPPY: Oh yeah, just wait. Plenny, plenny crabs, all kinds.

LEE: How you found dis place?

ZIPPY: My cousin brought me.

SHIMA: Real peaceful.

ZIPPY: We gotta tie up da aku heads to da nets. See, like dis.

SHIMA: Chee, da messy, eh. Ben, do 'um for me, since you going be one doctor.

LEE: Wat? All dis blood? 'S nuttin'. Dig in, man. Aeh, so long as not your blood, wat you care.

(The three mime everything, including throwing out the nets and pulling in the crabs. ZIPPY is the first to throw out his net into the large pond.)

ZIPPY: Okay, mine is out. Now da net going settle to da bottom, and we gotta wait for da crabs to crawl in.

SHIMA: Stink, man. Gotta use aku heads? How 'bout marshmallows, get plenny in da car.

ZIPPY: No, aku heads da best. All da blood and smell attract da crabs.

LEE: I going t'row mine out now.

ZIPPY: Yeah, good. Wait, go ova dat side little bit, away from mine, spread 'um out.

LEE: Aeh, bossy, eh, dis guy.

(LEE throws his net.)

ZIPPY: Let's go, Shima, let's go.

SHIMA: Aeh, aeh, aeh, take it easy, dis fish head still alive.

(SHIMA finally heaves his net.)

ZIPPY: Now we gotta wait little while.

LEE: 'S easy, real easy. I need dis time to rest. Man, I been going like crazy this year. Finally we going graduate.

SHIMA: How come Harvard wen' accept one slacka like you?

LEE: I dunno but I get 'um in black and white. Welcome, honored student, to da hallowed halls of ivy.

ZIPPY: Scary, eh? Harvard. Chee, one million miles away.

LEE: Nah, no sweat. Russ, you going UCLA, right?

SHIMA: California, here I come.

ZIPPY: Good old UH, 's where I going. We go UH, Russ.

SHIMA: Da Mainland schools wen' accept you too, Zip, we go.

ZIPPY: Too many haoles on da Mainland.

LEE: You sure you no like go? Learn from da haoles, learn da Mainland style.

ZIPPY: No mo' nuttin' I like on da Mainland. Da Mainland waste time.

LEE: I going love it up dere. Too many Orientals in Hawai'i. You no can stand out. Everybody look da same. I gotta be da only one different from everybody else.

ZIPPY: You funny, Ben. Wen you go to da Mainland, everybody going stare at you.

LEE: Let 'um look. I no care. Dey see me, one Oriental, dey going remembal me. 'S right, eh, Russ? 'S why you gotta go to da Mainland too. You just like me.

SHIMA: I dunno. Hawai'i is good too, in its way.

LEE: You bugga. You already can talk like one haole now.

SHIMA: If I like.

LEE: Yeah, if you like. You know we gotta be like da haoles or we not going learn. Even Miss Gray told us dat. She said if we talk pidgin English, everybody going laugh at us. If dey laugh at me, I going punch 'um out.

SHIMA: Ben, you smarta dan me, you da valedictorian. Not me. You can keep up wit' da haoles up dere. 'S da main ting. You no need worry about failing. You know you going make A's at Harvard.

LEE: Dat ain't no guarantee, man. And who told dem make me valedictorian? I not going give one speech. Whose bright idea was dat da valedictorian gotta stand up and address da graduating class?

SHIMA: 'S tradition.

LEE: Bullshit wit' tradition.

ZIPPY: Ben, you just said you like stand out from everybody else.

LEE: Yeah, but I no like stand out if I sound like one asshole. Shima, you gotta give da speech for me. You know, like one haole.

SHIMA: Forget it. You go up dere and take your medicine. Me and Zip going be laughing it up listening to you.

ZIPPY: Make ass, man, make ass.

LEE: You guys laugh now but just wait, just wait.

SHIMA: Too bad we cannot stay in high school foreva.

LEE: I cannot wait to get out on my own. I tired listening to my muddah and faddah telling me wat I gotta do. I like freedom.

ZIPPY: Just tink. Dis going be da first time we going be separated in ten years.

SHIMA and LEE: Yeah.

(There is a moment of silence while the boys are deep in thought.)

ZIPPY: Aeh, I tink da crabs ready.

(He pulls in his net.)

LEE: Wat dat? I tink I see someting.

SHIMA: Yeah, yeah, crabs, man. One, two, look, look, four, four crabs in one net!

(ZIPPY dumps his catch into an aluminum tub.)

ZIPPY: Okay, you guys, pull in your nets. Pull 'um in fast, no give da crabs chance to jump out.

(SHIMA *pulls in his net.*)

SHIMA: Aeh, look. Dere one crab, wait, two, two different kine.

ZIPPY: See da reddish-brown one? 'S one Hawaiian crab. Watch it, no tip 'um ova. Okay, okay, good, good, easy.

SHIMA: Aeh, dis betta dan fishing.

(LEE *is pulling his net.*)

LEE: Wassamadda wit' mine? Damn, wat I get out dere? One rock, one big lousy rock.

ZIPPY: Dat ain't no rock, man. 'S one crab. Keep pulling, no stop!

LEE: Wat?

SHIMA (*overlapping*): You sure 's one crab?

ZIPPY: Yeah, yeah, pull, pull.

LEE (*overlapping*): One big bamboola! Wow!

ZIPPY (*overlapping*): Easy, easy, no tip ova da net. Watch out, wait, okay, okay.

(*All three laugh, yell, jump around, having a good time.* ZIPPY *turns over the crab into the tub.*)

SHIMA: Oh man, da pinchas huge.

LEE: Look at da size of da body!

ZIPPY: 'S one giant Samoan crab! Dis must be da granddaddy of 'um all.

SHIMA: Da attack of da crab monsta!

LEE: Aeh, da bugga had some good old times, but dose days are ova!

ZIPPY: I told you guys, eh, I told you! T'row out da nets again and we start all ova.

SHIMA: Let's get dose crabs!

LEE: Crab salad tonight!

SHIMA: Crab in black bean sauce!

ZIPPY: Crab guts on rice!

(*Buddy Holly's "Oh Boy" plays as the boys throw out their nets.* LEE *runs off with the tub as* ZIPPY *and* SHIMA *pull in their nets. The song continues as the two boys exit.*)

Scene 7

(*Lights up on a spot where* LEE *enters, wearing a black graduation outfit.*)

LEE: And so I say to da Class of 1958, we are da future stars of da Territory of Hawai'i. Let us look to da future, to da brave new world of discovery and achievement. A world of wonda and challenge and, yes, even adversity. But we will triumph and make our alma mater proud as we take our place on da honor roll of responsible citizens of da world. I t'ank you for your kine attention and wish you all, my fellow classmates, a happy and prosperous tomorrow.

(A loud cheer erupts from the seniors. A male chorus sings "You'll Never Walk Alone." The three boys enter in casual clothes as the song ends.)

SHIMA: Well, we graduated.

ZIPPY: Da world still rotating.

LEE: So wat we going do tonight to celebrate?

ZIPPY: You guys like go McCully Chop Sui get someting to eat?

SHIMA: Or we can go to KC Drive-in. I wonda if Asato working tonight. Maybe we can talk wit' him in da parking lot.

LEE: Yeah, we go KC eat and see Asato. Although I radda go see Ruby. Rememba her? Last year?

ZIPPY: Sharon was nice too. She stay at UH now.

LEE: Wat about your girl, Shima? Wat her name?

SHIMA: She not my girl. Her name was Donna.

LEE: Da one wit' pimples.

SHIMA: She neva had pimples.

ZIPPY: I tink Ruby went school in da East.

SHIMA: She wouldn't go out wit' Ben anyway afta wat he did to her.

LEE: Wat I did?

SHIMA: She probably still mad at you for burying your face in her crotch.

LEE: Aeh, was not her crotch. And I neva bury my face in. Chee, dis bugga. My head wen' slip.

ZIPPY: We go drive around little while.

LEE: Yeah, we go. You drive.

ZIPPY: You trust me?

LEE: Of course. You not one high school kid anymo'. You now in dat ozone between high school and college.

SHIMA: Maybe we can find someting interesting to do.

LEE: Sit in da front, Russ. I be da back-seat driva.

SHIMA: You sure?

LEE: Yeah, I no like sit up front. 'S da death seat.

(*The boys arrange their cubes and sit as if in a car.* LEE *brings out three party horns and hands them around.*)

ZIPPY: Where you got dis from?

LEE: My sista's kid had one birt'day party so I wen' cacaroach t'ree. Clean. Unused.

(LEE *sticks his head out of the "car" and blows the horn long and hard. He laughs hysterically.*)

SHIMA: Where you going, Zip?

ZIPPY: We go down Kalakaua.

SHIMA: 'S good. Give da tourists a t'rill.

LEE: Where da haole coeds? Here I am, honey, I am your slave.

(*He continues laughing.*)

SHIMA: Wassamadda wit' you? You acting like you drunk.

ZIPPY: Yeah and we neva even drink.

LEE: No can help. I get drunk on air.

SHIMA: Aeh, okay, we on Kalakaua.

ZIPPY: Dere some girls on my side.

(*All three blow their horns, long and loud.*)

LEE: Happy New Year!

ZIPPY: Mele Kalikimaka!

SHIMA: Hauoli Makahiki Hou!

LEE: Hi, honey! Gimme a kiss! I love you! My name is Russell Shima.

SHIMA: Aeh, wat you saying? Make ass, you bugga!

(SHIMA, *in trying to get at* LEE *in the back seat, bumps against* ZIPPY.)

ZIPPY: Watch out, you guys, I almost wen' in da odda lane.

SHIMA: How we put up wit' him all dese years?

ZIPPY: No ask me. I figga he was like one lost poi dog. Somebody hadda be nice to him.

LEE: Hi, sweetie, where you from? Wanna fool around? My phone numba is 55–263.

SHIMA: Aeh, you bugga, 's my numba. No stop, Zip, keep going, go, go! Make ass, dis guy.

ZIPPY: Ben, she was one fifty-year-old tourist.

LEE: So? Aeh, you guys, I get da mean feeling dis going be da last time I going feel like one kid.

SHIMA: I doubt it.

LEE: I mean it. Da kid days going be ova from tonight. Afta dat, cold reality. Da brave new world awaits and we—

SHIMA: Da bugga giving his valedictorian address again. Lee, no torture us again. Once was enough.

LEE: Shima, was good, eh, da speech. Come on, you da speech guy. Was good, eh?

SHIMA: Yeah, yeah, was good. Your parents were really happy.

LEE: I was in a fog, man. I neva know wat I was saying. Dis is it. No mo' high school. No mo' Hawai'i. Freedom.

SHIMA: You not free yet. We still get four years of college. And you get med school, intern kine of shit, and I dunno wat else. Dis is just your beginning.

LEE: Shima, you killjoy bugga. Dis is wen da boy turns into a man. Hi, honey! How you? Aloha! I love you!

(The sound of a car revving up on ZIPPY's side.)

SHIMA: Zip, I tink da guy like drag.

LEE: Aeh, we owe you money o' wat? Aeh, brah, you like drag? Scared o' wat?

ZIPPY: Shaddup, Ben.

LEE: 'S one real jalopy you get dere. You no can do shit!

(More sounds of a car revving its engine.)

Give 'um da gas, Zippy. Give 'um plenny. Aeh, brah, wen da light turns green we go, okay? You hear dat, Zip. Go full blast. No give mercy. Dis black beauty can take it.

ZIPPY: I dunno how drag.

LEE: Shaddup, shaddup, you can. Hit da gas, work da clutch, bam into second and give 'um everyting into t'ird!

ZIPPY: I no can, I no can! We go change seats!

SHIMA: Too late, da light turning yellow!

ZIPPY: Ah, shit!

LEE: Get ready! Get ready! GO!!! Ya muddaaahhh!!!

(The sound of screeching tires and hot engines. The race is on.)

LEE: Get 'um, get 'um! Yeah, yeah!

SHIMA: Go, go! Go, Zippy, go! Neck and neck, you bugga!

LEE *(to the other car)*: Ya muddah! Ya muddah! We going beat da shit outta you!!

(The sound of a pure jet engine, it seems. And the black beauty roars forward. Both SHIMA *and* LEE *are halfway out of the car, looking back and giving the middle finger salute in the air.)*

SHIMA: You did it, Zip, you did it!

(Laughter erupts with cheers.)

ZIPPY: Look out!

*(*ZIPPY *turns the wheel, left, right, left, right.)*

SHIMA: Da tree! Left!

*(*ZIPPY *swerves left in time, burning tires as the car screeches to a stop. All three lunge forward and bounce back. There is a long pause of relief.)*

LEE: Man, I tought dat was it.

SHIMA: I saw da headlines. T'ree honor students die in wreck on graduation night.

LEE: Benjamin Gee Tim Lee cut down in da prime of life. He was destined for greatness. Wat a waste of a true genius.

ZIPPY: Was one cat on da road.

*(*LEE *grabs* ZIPPY *by the shoulders.)*

LEE: Next time run ova da cat. Get plenny cats, only t'ree of us.

SHIMA: Well, dat was our t'rill for da night.

ZIPPY: Ho, dat was someting, eh. Good fun. Look, I get chicken skin.

SHIMA: I going always rememba dis night. Win one drag race and almost die because of one cat. T'ree guys hanging out togedda to da end. I wonda wat going be like twenty years from now? I hope no change.

LEE: Twenty years. 1978. We going be t'irty-eight den.

ZIPPY: T'irty-eight? 'S old, man.

SHIMA: Farewell, good world. 'Tis a grand time ye gave us mere mortals. We pray your kindness extends into the future of your grateful inhabitants.

ZIPPY: Who said dat? Shakespeare?

SHIMA: I said dat.

LEE: You guys, I wen' just make up my mind.

SHIMA: Wat?

LEE: I going put you guys in my will.

ZIPPY: Wat you talking about?

LEE: I not going forget my buddies.

SHIMA: Wait, I know wat you mean. We wen' almost die togedda, but we wen' live. Dat was da sign. We gotta stick togedda, no matta wat. Friends foreva.

(*SHIMA extends his hands, palms down.*)

ZIPPY: Friends foreva.

(*ZIPPY places his hands on SHIMA's.*)

LEE: Friends foreva.

(*LEE puts his hands on top of ZIPPY's. Then ZIPPY and LEE exit. SHIMA addresses the audience.*)

SHIMA: Well, see you in twenty years. Or twenty minutes if you like. Goodbye, 1958. Goodbye, youth and innocence and high jinks. Look out, 1978!

(*SHIMA runs off. Blackout.*)

END OF ACT ONE

Act Two

Scene 1

(*SHIMA enters and addresses the audience.*)

SHIMA: Well, twenty years have passed. Benjamin Lee, Zippy Ching, and I went our separate ways in school and life. There were five-, ten- and fifteen-year class reunions, but we never attended, even though Zippy was in Hawai'i all this time. But the twentieth reunion, well, that's a real milestone. You attended yours, didn't you? At age thirty-eight, you just had to go back and see how your classmates had fared in the circus of life. Were they clowns or acrobats? A ringmaster or the guy who sweeps up behind elephants? To be frank, the twenty years are a blur to me. I was very insular. I found real life boring so I sought out dark sanctums of fantasy. I didn't pay attention to the historical events unfolding around me. One big thing, though, the Class of 1958 went in and out of the army before the Vietnam War got really bloody. Except Ben was in Vietnam, but you'll hear about that later. Oh, oh, I hear somebody coming. See you later.

(*SHARON enters as SHIMA exits. She's well dressed in a stylish muumuu. She inspects the living room, making sure everything is in its place.*)

SHARON: Roland, hurry up, your friend Ben going be here soon.

ZIPPY *(offstage)*: Yeah, yeah, where I leave my—

SHARON: Too bad he neva come for dinna.

ZIPPY *(offstage)*: Wat?

SHARON: I said . . . neva mind. *(She sits and practices several poses.)* Aeh, Ben, howzit, long time no see. No, no. Oh, how do you do, Ben. So nice to see you again after all these years. *(She extends her arm in greeting, smiles. ZIPPY comes out and watches.)* Oh, why, thank you. Oh, oh, please. Beautiful? Me?

(She laughs daintily. ZIPPY approaches her quietly.)

ZIPPY: Wat you doing?

SHARON *(startled)*: Why you sneak up on me for?

ZIPPY: I neva sneak—

SHARON: Walk mo' loud next time. You always walk loud, why you walk so soft dis time?

ZIPPY: Wat, I just walk da ordinary way I always walk.

SHARON: No make excuses. And wat you doing wearing dat?

(ZIPPY is wearing a humorous Hawaiian T-shirt with a nostalgic theme.)

ZIPPY: I like show Ben dis. He going crack up wen he see 'um.

SHARON: Roland, you not one kid anymo'. Go change 'um.

ZIPPY: No, I like show Ben.

SHARON: No, Ben not interested in da kine, you said so yourself. He so haolefied now.

ZIPPY: Yeah, compared to high school days. Like day and night. But cannot help, eh, he was on da East Coast all dis time—twenty years already.

SHARON: So dat's why, change your shirt.

ZIPPY: Okay, okay, chee, I no can get some fun o' wat?

(ZIPPY exits. SHARON fusses with herself while looking in a "mirror." The doorbell rings.)

SHARON: Roland, da doorbell!

ZIPPY *(offstage)*: Go answer 'um!

SHARON: But 's Ben.

ZIPPY *(offstage)*: So wat?

SHARON: You betta go or I not going play in bed wit' you tonight.

ZIPPY *(emerging)*: Cheeee.

(SHARON *exits as* ZIPPY *opens the door.* LEE *appears with a pretty box of chocolates.*)

ZIPPY: Aeh, Ben, how's da boy!

LEE: Zippy! Hey, all right! You looking good, Zip, real good.

ZIPPY: You neva change so much.

LEE: I take care of myself, you know. Watch my diet, exercise.

ZIPPY: No wonda you look so sharp. I betta do da same ting. Come inside, Sharon waiting. Sharon! Where she went? Sharon.

(SHARON *floats out ever so elegantly.*)

SHARON: Oh, hello, Ben, so nice to see you again after all these years.

LEE: Sharon, you look more beautiful today than you did in high school. Zippy's a lucky guy.

SHARON: Oh, what a sweet thing to say. Did you hear that, Roland dear?

LEE: Hope you like chocolates?

(*He hands her the box.*)

SHARON: Oh sure, we love them, thank you.

LEE: I was in Zurich a few days ago and I knew I was coming back for the reunion, so I bought it especially for you.

SHARON: Oh thank you, my goodness, you didn't have to, really.

LEE: Liqueur chocolates. Excellent chocolate.

SHARON: Oh, I'm sure. We get tired of eating chocolate-covered macadamia nuts. This is very special.

ZIPPY: Sit down, Ben, relax.

LEE: Yes, thank you.

(*All sit.* LEE *looks around.*)

ZIPPY: Ah, you want someting to drink? Coffee, wine, soda? We get everyting.

LEE: No, nothing right now. I just had dinner with some executives of this company. I'm sort of combining business with pleasure. Only way I could make this trip, just so busy, you know.

ZIPPY: Yeah, yeah. (*Pause.*) Oh, I know wat. I go get da cheese and crackers.

SHARON: No, you stay and talk.

ZIPPY: No, no, I come right back.

(ZIPPY *exits.*)

LEE: Sharon, you have a lovely home.

SHARON: Oh, thank you. Roland really works hard. He's a pretty good husband.

LEE: I think of the three guys, Zippy was always the one who was going to make a good husband. Russell and I were a little screwy.

SHARON: You guys talked about things like that in high school? Marriage and finding a wife?

LEE: No, we were too busy fooling around.

SHARON: Lots of girls, yeah.

LEE: No, we didn't have much time for girls.

SHARON: I know. Roland said you were the valedictorian of the class.

LEE: He mentioned that? Those were the days.

(ZIPPY returns with a tray of cheese and crackers.)

ZIPPY: Ben, try dis cheese first. Ono. Flavored wit' Portogee sausage.

LEE: No kidding.

(He munches on the cheese.)

ZIPPY: See da tings you miss not living in Hawai'i?

LEE: Where the kids?

ZIPPY: We sent 'um to summa camp. Get 'um outta our hair little while.

SHARON: Roland, not dat. It's a church camp. Out by Mokuleia. Geoffrey and Matthew love it.

LEE: How old are they now?

ZIPPY: Ten and eight. Getting sassy, dey like talk back.

SHARON: You don't act like a father, dat's why. He acts more like a pal or buddy.

ZIPPY: Cannot help. Ben, you know wat? I took da boys crabbing once. Rememba?

LEE: Yeah, that was great.

ZIPPY: Da kids neva enjoy so dat was it. Maybe dey was too young. Neva get too many crabs too. Not da same like before.

LEE: By the way, we're meeting Russ tomorrow?

ZIPPY: Right. Sharon, dis da first time da t'ree of us going be back togedda since 1958.

SHARON: I know. How many times you told me.

ZIPPY: Ben, you know Russell comes back to Hawai'i once in a while, not like you.

LEE: I've been busy. Business, travel. I didn't have time for Hawai'i.

SHARON: Well, now that you're back, I hope you return more often.

LEE: Maybe, never can tell.

ZIPPY: Sharon, you ready?

SHARON: Now? Maybe later.

ZIPPY: No shame. You da one wen' teach me and den. Aeh, Ben, I get one surprise for you. Try wait, try wait. I get 'um all ready.

(*ZIPPY exits quickly.*)

SHARON: He's been working on it just for you.

(*ZIPPY returns after turning on a cassette recorder.*)

ZIPPY: Okay, okay, watch dis.

(*SHARON and ZIPPY are poised and ready as Buddy Holly's "Ready Teddy" begins. They go into the bop.*)

LEE: Zippy! You can dance the fast ones!

(*Lights go down on the scene.*)

Scene 2

(*Lights up on SHIMA pacing at another part of the stage. ZIPPY enters.*)

ZIPPY: Aeh, Shima-san, you bugga.

SHIMA: Zippy, get your ass ova here. I no can wait all day. How you?

ZIPPY: Same old ting.

SHIMA: Looks like Civil Service agree wit' you.

ZIPPY: Can't beat it. Aeh, I ain't one peon anymore. I supervise lotta people.

SHIMA: Sure, afta all da years you put in. Ben coming, eh?

ZIPPY: You know Ben, always late as usual.

SHIMA: And wat? We going eat lunch someplace?

ZIPPY: Yeah. Wisteria restaurant.

SHIMA: Okay, good. Why you pick da Natatorium for us to meet?

ZIPPY: We used to hang out here and San Souci (*pronounces it Suzi*) Beach sometimes, so I figga good time to come back and see da old hunting grounds.

SHIMA: Sentimental bugga, eh, you. You saw our initials—still on da cannon.

ZIPPY: Who da sentimental bugga now?

SHIMA: Checking 'um out for posterity. How many years our initials been dere now? Someday either da cannon will be gone or our initials will be gone.

ZIPPY: You still reviewing movies for da newspaper?

SHIMA: Yeah, eight years now.

ZIPPY: You no get tired, see so many movies?

SHIMA: No, 's my job. We used to see lotta movies wen we were kids. Hawaii Theater, Liberty Theater, no forget dat.

ZIPPY: Yeah, yeah, I hardly go nowadays. No mo' time. Too busy working six days a week, lotta overtime. Not easy being one personnel manager. People like complain about deir bosses. No mo' end. Headache, man.

SHIMA: But worth it, eh. You get two boys continue on da Ching name, one nice wife to take care of you, cook ono kaukau. No can ask for more dan dat.

ZIPPY: No kid yourself, man. It's tough. Sometimes I like get away, just by myself. Rest da body little bit.

SHIMA: Come to L.A. I take you to Vegas.

ZIPPY: I wish. But you know me. If I lose five, six hundred dollars gambling, I going tink, I coulda bought one color TV or save da money so Sharon can buy one extra freezer to put in da garage.

SHIMA: Da life and times of a dedicated family man.

ZIPPY: You know wat? One night I was home alone. Sharon took da kids to her muddah's. So I took one long hot bath. Turn off da light, you know, close da door, and just relax in da tub in da dark. Was so good I wen' fall asleep. So I neva hear Sharon come home. She go to da bathroom, turn on da light and see me in da tub. She scream her head off. She tought I was dead. Scare da hell outta me. I told her, "No do like dat, you almost give me heart attack." And she tell me, "Who give who heart attack? Next time you tell me you going sleep in da tub wit' da lights out!" Russ, whose fault was, mine or hers?

SHIMA: Was nobody's fault. You lucky you get somebody worry about you.

ZIPPY: Wait, 's not all. She always tell me, "Put down da toilet seat afta you shishi." You know why she say dat? Because one night she get up to go to da bathroom and wen she wen' sit down, she sink down in da bowl because da seat was up. Ho, she was mad like hell. You tink I shoulda told her, if I gotta put da seat down, den you gotta pull da seat up wen you finish.

SHIMA: No, you betta off if you just shut up and let her have da last word.

ZIPPY: Aeh, wat about you? Good, you know, married life. Wen you going settle down?

SHIMA: No luck, man. I tink wen I'm forty-five, I'll probably marry a thirty-seven-year-old divorcee wit' two kids who will hate my guts.

ZIPPY: Life is hard, yeah. So how long you going be one movie critic?

SHIMA: As long as da newspaper pays me.

ZIPPY: Good job you get, eh. Not like one real job. Dey pay you to see movies. I tought you was going be one businessman or one school-teacher.

SHIMA: Funny, eh. 'S wat happen wen I wen' to UCLA. Changed my major to cinema. You know I'm writing a book titled *The Great Ladies of the Cinema.*

ZIPPY: No kidding. Who in da book?

SHIMA: Lillian Gish, Mary Pickford, Greta Garbo, Myrna Loy . . .

ZIPPY: 'S all da old ones. Wat about Doris Day? Or maybe . . .

SHIMA: Well, she was good for da kine of movies she made, but you know who was great and underappreciated?

ZIPPY: Ah, Debbie Reynolds?

SHIMA: Ginger Rogers. Especially in the Astaire-Rogers musicals of the thirties. Everybody praises Astaire, but Ginger was really special.

ZIPPY: Yeah?

SHIMA: *Top Hat* was Astaire's best, but *Swing Time* was Ginger's best movie musical.

ZIPPY: I neva even saw dose movies.

SHIMA: No other actress, past or present, can match Ginger Rogers for her all-around talent of singing, dancing, comedic flair, and dramatic honesty.

ZIPPY: Who said dat?

SHIMA: Me, I said that.

ZIPPY: Oh, I tought was one expert o' someting.

SHIMA: Aeh, I'm the expert.

ZIPPY: Oh you! Oh yeah, yeah, 's right, you da expert.

SHIMA: She's great, beautiful, sexy, lovable, funny, touching, sensitive—
  (*LEE enters.*)

LEE: Aeh, who is this woman, I gotta meet her. Shima, Shima, how you doing?

SHIMA: Ben, haven't seen you in a few years, eh.

LEE: Yeah, we gotta get together more often on the Mainland.

ZIPPY: Ben, you checked out our initials on da cannon?

LEE: No, why? Still there?

ZIPPY: Of course.

LEE: What can I say, I'm speechless.

ZIPPY: I rememba wen da Natatorium had some great races wen I was one kid.

LEE: The great stone palace. They gotta tear down this thing, build something useful.

SHIMA: Nothing doing, this is a historic landmark. Preserve it.

LEE: I never liked swimming in there. San Souci Beach was better. When I go back to the Waikiki Sheraton, I think I'll go lie down on the beach.

ZIPPY: I tought you was at your folks' house.

LEE: Had to get out. My mother kept bugging me. Why did I give up my medical practice? Why? Why? Then my father had to sound off. That was it. Pack it up, get out, shut the door. You know the thing wrong with parents? We grow up, we change, but they never change. They still have these old, tired ideas about what is important. And they can't see what we see.

SHIMA: Well, you know, all through high school you talked about going to med school.

LEE: Only because my parents wanted me to.

ZIPPY: Boy, you sounded like you really wanted to be one doctor. Sure fooled me.

LEE: I was a good actor. Russ, maybe I should've gone into acting.

SHIMA: No, no. Terrible profession for an Asian American. No good roles, only small parts with no meat. Very demeaning. Be happy on Wall Street as a stock analyst.

ZIPPY: Wat your specialty?

LEE: My expertise is in the medical field and pharmaceutical drug companies.

ZIPPY: Any hot tips?

LEE: Buy Bristol-Meyers. Good management, good dividend. Can't go wrong.

SHIMA: You know when you visited me in L.A., how come you didn't say anything?

LEE: Tell you what? That I didn't want to be a doctor anymore? No big deal.

SHIMA: But the very next year, you quit doctoring.

LEE: I like my present career. Make a lot of money in my job.

ZIPPY: I can ask how much?

LEE: Six figures.

ZIPPY: Dat much? I gotta raise my son to be one stock analyst too.

SHIMA: Money's not everything, Zip.

ZIPPY: But my boy Geoff like be one TV repairman. I gotta change his mind for him.

SHIMA: Just make sure he doesn't go into engineering. No let him be like Spencer Kamiya. Da bugga stuck in L.A. He really wants to come back to Hawai'i, but the job is on the Mainland.

LEE: I never liked the weather in Honolulu. Too humid, too same. No real change in the seasons. Boring, hot, muggy. Saps your energy. That's why people in Hawai'i move so slow.

ZIPPY: Just my speed.

LEE: Zip, come visit me in New York. The city makes you feel alive. Things are always happening. Busy people walking the streets, a river of humanity flowing along Fifth Avenue, Madison Avenue, Park Avenue, Central Park. We stop along the way and buy hot dogs from street vendors. We go to world-class museums during the day and Broadway shows at night. Lunch at Lindy's, dinner at Sardi's. What do you say?

ZIPPY: Hmmm, I too busy. Get lotta tings happening here too, you know.

LEE: Like what?

ZIPPY: Ah, I get dates for you and Russ.

SHIMA: What?

LEE: Dates, what kind dates? The kind you eat or the kind you take out?

ZIPPY: Guess.

SHIMA: You gotta be kidding.

ZIPPY: I hadda do it, I had to. Sharon wen' blackmail me.

LEE: No blind dates. I gave that up years ago.

SHIMA: We too old for blind dates.

ZIPPY: Yeah, yeah, but dis not blind dates. You know da girls.

SHIMA: We know them?

LEE: Wait a minute, I don't know any local girls. I've been away twenty years.

ZIPPY: You tink I lie to you guys? Wen I say you know da girls, brah, you know da girls.

LEE: Let me think. The last local girl I took out was Margaret Leong. Not Margaret Leong?

ZIPPY: No.

LEE: Phew, that's good.

SHIMA: The last girl in Hawai'i I dated was Julie Yokoyama.

LEE: Yeah, Yokoyama Mama.

SHIMA: Not her?

ZIPPY: No.

LEE: Too bad.

SHIMA: What's this, too bad? You had the hots for her?

LEE: Yokoyama Mama had daikon legs and bow legs, what a combination.

SHIMA: You gotta be thinking about somebody else. Julie's legs were straight and skinny.

LEE: Oh yeah, oh yeah, good, good, tell yourself—

SHIMA: It's true.

ZIPPY: Aeh, aeh, you guys, try tink. Rememba Sharon's friends?

SHIMA: Sharon's friends?

ZIPPY: Rememba wen we first met dem at our junior dance? Rememba wen we took dem to Ala Moana Park for one picnic?

LEE: Her name was Ruby.

ZIPPY: And your girl's name was Donna.

SHIMA: She wasn't my girl. She not married yet?

ZIPPY: Dey both single.

SHIMA: Donna was too uptight. How could a girl with a warm name like Donna have such a cold personality?

ZIPPY: Aeh, Russ, Donna really wen' change.

SHIMA: Who said?

ZIPPY: Sharon.

SHIMA: No thanks.

ZIPPY: You gotta, or Sharon going kill me. Was her idea.

LEE: Zippy, Zippy, they're old now. Thirty-nine, right?

ZIPPY: Well, you t'irty-eight.

LEE: I take out women who are twenty-four or twenty-five, maybe twenty-six or twenty-seven.

ZIPPY: Kinna young, eh, for you, I mean.

LEE: Not haole girls. That's the only kind I date in New York. And the only girl I married was haole. Too bad we had to divorce. She was nice but . . .

ZIPPY: Well, too late to back out. Sharon already told dem you going take dem out.

SHIMA: And they said okay?

ZIPPY: I tink Ruby and Donna really like see you again.

LEE: But how come they're not married?

ZIPPY: Dey can say da same ting about you guys.

LEE: That's just it. We're guys, you know, guys. Guys need time to sort things out and have some fun.

SHIMA: Zip, I dunno how to thank you.

ZIPPY: Aeh, no sweat, brah, anytime.

LEE: Hot today, eh, Zip. I think you gotta cool off.

SHIMA: Yeah, good time for a swim.

(LEE *and* SHIMA *have* ZIPPY *by the arms. They rush him toward the exit.*)

ZIPPY: No, no, not wit' my clothes on. Aaaaahhhh!

(*Lights go down and there is a loud splash.*)

Scene 3

(*Lights up as* SHARON, RUBY, *and* DONNA *enter* SHARON's *living room.* SHARON *wears a simple muumuu;* DONNA *is smartly dressed in a pantsuit and wears no glasses;* RUBY *looks sharp in a tasteful dress.*)

SHARON: Exciting, yeah? You going meet Ben and Russell afta all dese years.

RUBY: No, it's embarrassing, it's traumatic. How could you?

SHARON: Ssshhh, not me. It was Roland's idea.

DONNA: You sure they said they wanted to take us out?

SHARON: Yeah, honest. Dey tought it was a great idea. 'S wat Roland said. You shoulda seen Ben, he was drooling at da mout' wen Roland told him you were available.

RUBY: Available?

SHARON: Ah . . . unoccupied? Unattached?

RUBY: Sharon, if you lying . . .

SHARON: I promise, I promise. Ask Roland. *(Sweetly)* Roland, Roland. *(Now sternly)* Roland!

(ZIPPY enters, chewing on something.)

ZIPPY: Wat?

SHARON: Ben and Russell said dey really want to take out Ruby and Donna, yeah?

(She gives ZIPPY the eye, gesturing and trying to coax him to go along.)

ZIPPY: Oh . . . yeah, yeah, 's right. I told dem you girls really look terrific.

RUBY: You didn't.

ZIPPY: I did. But 's right. You two really look nice. No worry, go out. Going be good fun.

DONNA: Ruby, what we gonna do?

RUBY: Go out with them, I guess.

DONNA: Where they taking us?

ZIPPY: Well, not going be one double date.

DONNA: It's not?

ZIPPY: No. Dey each get deir own idea about where to go.

SHARON: Okay, honey, t'anks, you can go back eat.

(ZIPPY exits with a thumb-up sign.)

DONNA: I hope he's not gonna take me to a movie. You know I don't like movies.

RUBY: He'll probably take you to dinner and a nightclub in Waikiki.

DONNA: Oh yeah?

SHARON: Yeah. And you know wat? If I wasn't married, I could go wit' you guys.

DONNA: You take my place then, and I'll stay with Roland.

SHARON: Oh no, bumbai you steal my honey away.

DONNA: Sharon, you know me.

SHARON: I know. I just kidding. You worry too much, Donna. Have a good time. Laugh, laugh, and don't stop laughing. I know going be hard 'cause Russell has no sense of humor.

DONNA: He's gonna think it's funny I never got married.

RUBY: Well, he never got married, either.

DONNA: It's different with men.

RUBY: Times have changed. Women have more freedom today.

SHARON: Ruby's right. You gotta loosen up little bit.

DONNA: What if he asks why I never married?

RUBY: He won't ask. Don't be silly. Oh, what the hell. Let's go and make the best of it.

SHARON: Yeah, good. You lucky, you know. All I going do tonight is stay home and watch TV wit' Roland.

(*SHARON frowns, and* RUBY *and* DONNA *give her gentle pats on the shoulder and say, "Aaawww." Lights out on the women.*)

Scene 4

(*Two spots of light hit downstage left and right. Rod Stewart's "Do Ya Think I'm Sexy" plays.* LEE *and* RUBY *take one spot,* SHIMA *and* DONNA *the other.*)

LEE: You know, the first time I met you was at a dance.

RUBY: I remember. 1957.

LEE: That's why I thought we'd go dancing tonight.

RUBY: Nice.

(LEE *and* RUBY *dance slowly in place to romantic music. Lights go down on them.*)

SHIMA: I hope you don't mind going to a movie.

DONNA: Oh no. I . . . like movies.

SHIMA: That's good. I got the newspaper here. Any particular movie you want to see?

DONNA: No, no, whatever you want. I don't care.

SHIMA: Let's see. *Midnight Express.* No, too raw for you, I think. *Coming Home.* Hmmm, no. *Deer Hunter* at the Kuhio Theater. Nah. Wait, here's the perfect movie. I think you'll like it. *An Unmarried Woman.*

DONNA: *An Unmarried Woman? An Unmarried Woman* is the perfect movie for me? I mean, what, because what, I . . .

SHIMA: Jill Clayburgh was great in the movie and . . . what? Did I say . . . no, no, I mean *Unmarried Woman* is not a perfect movie, period. It's flawed, I mean, terribly flawed. Oh, look! *Heaven Can Wait* with Warren Beatty. Let's see that. I saw it already, but it's fun, a fun movie.

(*Lights down on* DONNA *and* SHIMA. *Lights up on* SHARON *and* ZIPPY *upstage, watching TV.* ZIPPY *laughs, pointing at the TV set.* SHARON *is bored. Lights down on them, up on* LEE *and* RUBY.)

LEE: May I say you look beautiful tonight.

RUBY: You may.

LEE: And sexy.

RUBY: Sexy? A thirty-nine-year-old divorcee with ten pounds of rice bags under her eyes?

LEE: Uh-uh. All I see is perfection, from head to toe.

RUBY: It's funny seeing you again. Naturally, you've changed.

LEE: You mean I'm not a clumsy, seventeen-year-old virgin anymore. You've changed too. You look better today than you did in high school.

RUBY: Keep the compliments coming. It may get you somewhere.

(*LEE reacts with a smile. Lights down on them. Lights up on* DONNA *and* SHIMA *sitting in a theater watching the movie.* SHIMA *laughs and looks at* DONNA, *who has a glazed expression.*)

SHIMA: Donna?

DONNA: Yes?

SHIMA: Want popcorn or something?

DONNA: Oh no.

SHIMA: I can get you candy.

DONNA: No, thank you.

SHIMA: Soda?

DONNA: I'm not thirsty.

SHIMA: How do you like the movie so far?

DONNA: Oh, it's good.

SHIMA: Charles Grodin and Dyan Cannon are funny, huh?

DONNA: Oh yes. Which ones are they?

(*Lights down on them, up on* ZIPPY *and* SHARON. ZIPPY *laughs, elbows* SHARON. *Lights down. Lights up on* LEE *and* RUBY.)

LEE: The last time I saw you was at the beach. I got sick on cockroach stew and you were kind enough to lend me your lap as a pillow.

RUBY: Oh yeah, that's when you suddenly turned into a groundhog and tried to find something buried deep in my—

LEE: Whoa, whoa, I tried to what? You don't think I would, I, I, my head slipped.

RUBY: If you hadn't stopped, you might've found something you liked.

LEE: Ahhh . . . what did you say?

RUBY: Nothing.

(RUBY *smiles and moves in, pressing close to* LEE'S *body, head on his shoulder. His eyes widen and he is all smiles. Lights down. Lights up on* ZIPPY *and* SHARON. *She has her head on his shoulder.*)

ZIPPY: Sharon, you—

SHARON: Yes, honey?

ZIPPY: You can put your head up? Kinna heavy.

(SHARON *hits him in the stomach with a little pillow. Lights down, lights up on* LEE *and* RUBY *still dancing.*)

LEE: You know what you said . . .

RUBY: What did I say?

LEE: About finding something deep in your . . . you know.

RUBY: Isn't that true?

LEE: Well, yeah. But the question is: would you have let me have it?

RUBY: I was a little surprised then. But, after all, I was only in high school. I'm not in high school anymore.

LEE: Thank goodness for that.

RUBY: By the way, I like your leg-in technique.

LEE: My what?

RUBY: Your leg-in technique. Sharon told me all about it. Roland squealed.

LEE: Well, you know . . .

RUBY: I like it.

LEE: You do?

RUBY: Very effective.

LEE: It is?

RUBY: Hmmm, all that rubbing is making me so . . .

(LEE *smiles wickedly and they exit. Lights up brightly on* SHIMA *and* DONNA.)

SHIMA: Oh no. Now what?

DONNA: What happened?

SHIMA: Probably the film broke. Sorry about that.

DONNA: Oh no, it's not your fault.

SHIMA: Well, I'm glad you're enjoying the movie.

DONNA: Oh . . . yes.

SHIMA: I was afraid if I took you to a movie, you would think it was like a high school thing.

DONNA: Oh no, I, you know, it's, it's fine.

SHIMA: What movies have you seen lately?

DONNA: Lately? I've been so busy. I haven't seen many, not lately.

SHIMA: Ah, what're some of your all-time favorites?

DONNA: All-time favorites. Oh, I don't know. Ah, you love movies, don't you?

SHIMA: Oh yeah. In my job I see lots and lots of movies. New ones, old ones, good ones, bad ones. And I see some movies over and over again.

DONNA: Why? You know the story. It seems such a waste of time to see it again.

SHIMA: It's not a waste of time.

DONNA: Oh, I didn't mean a waste, really. I don't know what I meant. I'm sorry.

SHIMA: No, no, let me explain. You see new things in a movie every time it's run. And, of course, you can see a film so often it becomes a part of you. People say it's only a movie, but no, a movie can teach you, it can guide you in your everyday life. Movies are the conscience of our society.

DONNA: Oh, I didn't realize.

SHIMA: Most people don't. Now, can I ask you a question?

DONNA: A question? Me? What?

SHIMA: Well, tell me, how come you didn't—

DONNA: Get married?

SHIMA: What?

DONNA: Oh!

SHIMA: No, I was going to say, "How come you didn't eat much at dinner?" I thought maybe you were feeling sick.

DONNA: Yes, that's what I thought you were going to ask.

SHIMA *(overlapping, as lights dim)*: Oh good, the movie's starting again.
  (Lights down, lights up on SHARON *and* ZIPPY*.)*

ZIPPY: Sharon, I can feel da heat from your body.

SHARON *(snuggling even closer)*: Hmmmm, yeah.

ZIPPY: Too hot, you sitting too close.

SHARON: Nobody home but us, you know. Ruby and Donna out having a good time wit' Russell and Ben.

ZIPPY: I feel bad I hadda lie to dem.

SHARON: Who? Donna and Ruby?

ZIPPY: No, Russell and Ben.

SHARON: No worry, dey know know wat dey doing.

ZIPPY: Who? Russ and Ben?

SHARON: No, Donna and Ruby.

(SHARON *slips her hand behind the pillow that* ZIPPY *is holding in front of him. She strokes him slyly.*)

ZIPPY: Aeh, no do dat. You boddering me. I like see Mary Tyler Moore, my favorite show.

SHARON: I feel so lucky. I get one handsome, sexy husband. And poor Ruby is divorced. And Donna neva got married. And I hot, Roland.

ZIPPY: Go get da electric fan. And bring me some beef jerky and diet Pepsi.

SHARON: No.

ZIPPY: Wassamadda, I hungry.

SHARON: I hungry too.

ZIPPY: Okay den.

SHARON: Good, we go to da bedroom.

ZIPPY: But da beef jerky in da kitchen.

(*She takes the pillow and hits him over the head, then exits in a huff.* ZIPPY *watches her leave, then turns to the TV again, laughing. Lights down on* ZIPPY, *lights up on* LEE *and* RUBY *as they reenter.*)

LEE: Here we are. Wanna drink?

RUBY: Oh, you have a view of the mountains.

LEE: From the bedroom I have a view of the ocean.

RUBY: How about champagne?

LEE: Coming up. I'll get room service. Now tell me. Those lights out there. Where is that? I forget.

(*Lights down on them, lights up dimly on* DONNA *and* SHIMA *still watching the movie. He leans back, sneaks a peek at* DONNA *and tries to loosen up.* DONNA *has her right hand on her lap.* SHIMA *decides to put his hand on hers. As he moves his hand, she brings hers up to cover a cough. He has his hand on her lap instead. He's embarrassed; so is she. He pulls back his hand, mortified. Lights down, lights up on* ZIPPY *watching TV.*)

SHARON (*offstage, sweetly*): Honey, try come.

ZIPPY: Wat you like?

SHARON (*offstage*): I like show you someting.

ZIPPY: Show me wat?

SHARON (*offstage, sternly*): Try come and see, I said!

(*As ZIPPY exits, he continues to look back at the TV. Lights down, lights up on LEE and RUBY drinking champagne.*)

RUBY: I'm curious. Why'd you give up being a doctor?

LEE: Everybody wants to know that. Russ, Zippy, my mother, my father. It's a long story.

RUBY: I have all night.

LEE (*looking deeply into her eyes*): Okay. You I'll tell. And I'll keep it short. I was in Da Nang at the hospital. Patching up guys, losing guys. The war was going wild. I saw the faces, the bodies, and they just kept coming. No end in sight. I got sick of it.

RUBY: You did important work there. You must've saved a lot of lives.

LEE: All our young kids dying, and the Vietnamese people suffering so much. It changed my whole way of thinking. See, I like good times, laughs, parties, and spending money.

RUBY: I'm sure there're doctors who like the same things, but they don't quit.

LEE: But for me, when I got back to the States, I thought it all out. A doctor, a real doctor, should be like those from the country days. They made house calls. They took their pay in chickens or vegetables if they had to. Doctors should be poor but blessed by God for their unselfishness.

RUBY: Very idealistic, aren't you. But not realistic.

LEE: I didn't want to make money from patients dying under my care. I decided I wanted the finer things in life. And I wanted to make tons of money, but not from poor, suffering people. I wanted to make my fortune from rich, healthy people who can afford my expertise. So now I tell my clients what stocks to buy and they get rich from my advice. It's better that way. Everybody's happy.

RUBY: What makes you happy, that's the important thing.

LEE: See, money is not the root of all evil. Actually money can bring happiness. For example, someday I'll be a billionaire, I'll donate millions to charitable causes that help poor people. I'll feel good, everybody'll feel good. Yes, it's great to be rich.

(*Lights down; lights up on ZIPPY as he runs out in boxer shorts to look at the TV.*)

ZIPPY: Aaawww, you see! Da show ova! You make me miss Mary Tyler Moore.

SHARON (offstage): Honey, hurry up. No make me wait. I'm so hot. No be mean.

ZIPPY (beaming): Okay, okay.

(He stands and pounds his chest and gives out a Tarzan yell, then runs off. Lights down, lights up on SHIMA and DONNA.)

SHIMA: I hope you liked the movie.

DONNA: Oh, it was good.

SHIMA: Wanna go some place?

DONNA: Where?

SHIMA: Oh, I don't know. Depends on what you wanna do.

DONNA: I don't know.

SHIMA: We could stay here and see the movie again.

DONNA: Oh no! I mean . . .

SHIMA: I know. It would be a waste of time.

DONNA: It's not that, but . . . (He leans toward her to give her a kiss, but DONNA innocently turns her head away.) I wonder what Ruby and Ben are doing?

SHIMA: Ah, I think Ben said they would go back to his hotel room after dinner.

DONNA: Maybe the four of us could go somewhere.

SHIMA: I guess so.

(They exit. Lights up on ZIPPY and SHARON as they enter, arm in arm.)

SHARON: Okay, who was betta? Mary Tyler Moore or me?

ZIPPY: I dunno. I neva did it to Mary Tyler Moore.

(She tickles him.)

ZIPPY: I give up, I give up. You da best. You always da best.

SHARON: Oh, you didn't have to say dat. (She kisses him.) Come on, let's go! Round Two!

(She skips off. The smile on ZIPPY's lips fade to a frown. His shoulders droop, he turns to follow SHARON in tired, worn-out steps. He stops and turns.)

ZIPPY: Wait! I gotta have some beef jerky!

(He exits in the opposite direction. Lights up on LEE and RUBY.)

RUBY: I think it's time to see what's happening on the ocean.

LEE: Oh yeah?

RUBY: There's a full moon. We can probably see way out.

(As they are about to go, there is a knock on the door.)

LEE: Who could that be?

(SHIMA and DONNA enter.)

RUBY: Donna, what happened?

DONNA: Nothing. We took a chance you two were here.

(SHIMA and LEE move downstage.)

LEE: What the hell you doing here?

SHIMA: I thought maybe Donna and I could use your room.

LEE: You and Donna? What about me and Ruby?

SHIMA: I thought you'd be finished by now.

LEE: I didn't even start.

SHIMA: Good. I didn't want to interrupt something.

LEE: But you did interrupt. I'm going great with Ruby. You and Donna gotta go.

SHIMA: Why don't the four of us go out to eat?

LEE: I got a delicious dish right here. I don't have to go out.

SHIMA: How 'bout saimin at Likelike Drive-in?

LEE: Do me a favor. Take Donna and go. Any place. I'll pay you to go. How much do you want?

SHIMA: I don't know what to say to her. She's so shy she doesn't want to talk about herself. And I'm tired of talking about myself. I don't think she likes me.

LEE: She likes you, I can tell.

SHIMA: Don't give me that shit. I look at her and I think, she likes me, she doesn't like me, she likes me, she doesn't. I can't read her. I give up.

RUBY: Ben. Donna asked if we wanted to go out for some food, but I told her we had a big late dinner and we're not hungry.

LEE: That's right. Absolutely.

RUBY: So Donna and Russell have to go by themselves.

LEE: Yes, that's right. Too bad, too bad.

DONNA: Sorry we couldn't all go. It would've been nice.

LEE: Yeah, yeah, great double date. Maybe next time.

SHIMA: Okay. Have fun, you two.

LEE: We'll try. You too. Enjoy your saimin or whatever.

(SHIMA *and* DONNA *exit.* LEE *and* RUBY *embrace and kiss. Lights down.*)

Scene 5

(*Lights up as* ZIPPY *and* SHARON *enter. It is the next day.*)

ZIPPY: I betta not stick around, yeah. You girls like talk private.

SHARON: Yeah, I like hear all da dirt.

ZIPPY: You going tell me aftawards, eh?

SHARON: Of course. No mo' fun keep da secret all to myself.

ZIPPY: Good, good.

SHARON: But you gotta tell me wat da guys say.

ZIPPY: Every word.

(ZIPPY *exits as* DONNA *and* RUBY *enter.*)

RUBY: Where Roland going?

SHARON: Oh, he gotta go shopping for some tings. And I no like he hear all da juicy stuff you going tell me. So wat happen last night?

RUBY: You're not going to tell Roland, are you?

SHARON: Oooohh nnoooo. No can tell boys our secrets.

RUBY: You promise?

SHARON: Cross my heart and shut my mout'.

DONNA: Russell was nice.

SHARON: Nice? How nice? Good nice or bad nice?

DONNA: Good nice. He was a perfect gentleman.

SHARON: If he was a gentleman, he wasn't perfect. Gawd, dat Russell is so dull.

DONNA: We had a nice time. We had dinner at Wisteria, then went to see this movie, *Heaven Is Waiting.* Later we had saimin at Likelike.

SHARON: You don't like saimin.

DONNA: Well, I ate it.

SHARON: So you neva like make love wit' Russell all naked in bed?

DONNA: Sharon, you so embarrassing.

SHARON: Wat? I can picture you and Russell making love. Very natural.

DONNA: You can? No, no, erase that from your head right now. I don't want to be in your X-rated mind.

SHARON: So, Ruby, wat happen wit' you? He wen' try someting?

RUBY: No. But I did.

DONNA: Ruby!

SHARON: You? Oooooohhhhh, wat you did?

RUBY: I gave him the best sex he ever had.

SHARON: He was good in bed?

RUBY: He was fine. But I had better. Actually I'm sorry Ben's returning to the Mainland. I really liked him. But he has his own life in New York, and I'm no longer interested in living on the Mainland.

DONNA: Last night I said some things I shouldn't have. And I didn't say things I should have.

SHARON: Me too. I was pushing it wen I told Roland, "Round Two."

RUBY: Oh well, last night we just donated a tiny fraction of our lives as our good deed for 1978.

(*Lights down on the women.*)

Scene 6

(*Lights up brightly as* ZIPPY *enters in T-shirt and shorts, with rubber slippers. He carries an aluminum tub.*)

ZIPPY: Aeh, you guys, I know you tired from da reunion dinna last night, but 's no reason to drag your ass around. Let's go, da crabs waiting.

(SHIMA *and* LEE *enter, mime carrying crab nets.*)

LEE: Yeah, yeah, hold on, man, I got a hangover.

SHIMA: Good thing reunions happen every five or ten years.

ZIPPY: Rememba dis? Just us and da dumb crabs. 1958 all ova again.

SHIMA: Kaneko sure changed, eh?

LEE: I think he was an impostor. Nobody can change that much.

SHIMA: Was him. I asked him to laugh. Soon as he opened his mouth, I knew it was him.

LEE: Imagine, Kaneko, the owner of a trash hauling company in Portland, Oregon.

(*The guys mime tying aku heads to their nets.*)

SHIMA: Funny, the guy with the dirtiest mouth in the Class of '58 goes around picking up garbage.

ZIPPY: Yeah but he might be one millionaire.

SHIMA: He loves his *f*-words. Hauling garbage is the perfect job for him.

LEE: I gave him a parting shot. I said, "If you pick up rubbish for a living, why don't you clean the rubbish from your mouth?

ZIPPY: Aeh, da mean bugga, eh, you.

LEE: Nah, he thought it was funny. He just laughed. That Kaneko has a good sense of humor. If he can laugh at himself, he's all right.

SHIMA: How 'bout Harry Kondo and Michael Kim? I told them, "Come on, who are you really?"

LEE: Yeah, Harry and Mike. How come those guys turned out so ugly? I'm still as handsome as I was in high school, right?

SHIMA: Even prettier.

ZIPPY: Okay, my net going out.

LEE: Go, man, let 'um fly. (*ZIPPY "throws" out his net, followed by LEE, then SHIMA.*) Place hasn't changed much.

SHIMA: Zip, good idea you had coming back here.

ZIPPY: For old times, eh. Ben, how come you neva bring Ruby to da reunion dinna?

LEE: Ruby? No, she's a busy, independent woman. My kind of woman.

ZIPPY: Hear dat, Shima? Da bugga hooked, maybe.

LEE: No, not me.

ZIPPY: Come on, you can tell us.

LEE: Tell you what?

ZIPPY: About you and Ruby dat night, dat hot and sweaty night. Ruby told Sharon everyting. And Sharon told me. I wen' drag da secret outta her.

LEE: Told you what?

ZIPPY: Dat you and Ruby were burning da bed all night.

LEE: Ruby. That woman has no shame. She was great. Unbridled passion. Never had an Oriental woman make love like that. Real savage. I told her I wanted to take her back to New York with me. But she said she had enough of the Mainland. Hawai'i was where she wanted to stay. So that was quick. I can't stand the Islands, and she hates the Mainland.

SHIMA: Donna said anything to Sharon?

ZIPPY: No. Well, she said you were a perfect gentleman.

SHIMA: Yeah, I treated her with respect.

ZIPPY: But, you know, she said she really liked you.

SHIMA: She did? Why the hell didn't she show it? We could've had so much fun if she, she . . .

ZIPPY: 'S why hard, yeah.

LEE: Aeh, don't mope around all day, Shima, not good for the crabs.

SHIMA: Yeah, yeah, how 'bout the nets?

ZIPPY: Full of crabs, I bet.

LEE: Me first.

(LEE pulls in his net and it's empty.)

LEE: What happen? Nothing.

ZIPPY: Maybe da net was turned ova.

LEE: No, I did it right. I did my job.

ZIPPY: I try mine.

(ZIPPY pulls in his net. Nothing.)

SHIMA: How come, eh. Yours empty too.

(SHIMA tries his net.)

LEE: Zero. So we came here for nothing. I should've stayed in bed. What a dumb idea.

ZIPPY: You know, I tought for old times, you guys like come back again. You rememba, was good fun dat time.

LEE: Yeah, but we ain't kids anymore. I got better things to do.

ZIPPY: See da rubbish? Lotta people must be coming. Taking all da crabs. I going try da odda side. Try wait.

(ZIPPY exits.)

SHIMA: Don't make Zippy feel bad.

LEE: About what?

SHIMA: The crabs. Not his fault.

LEE: Yeah, he means well. Maybe I shouldn't have come back for the reunion. I got nothing in common with those guys. Hawai'i just doesn't do it for me anymore. Remember how badly we wanted to get to the Mainland. Hawai'i was too small to hold our ambitions.

SHIMA: Maybe we should've stayed in Hawai'i.

LEE: Nah, don't think that way. It's a trap, a nostalgic trap. Let's face it. We both belong on the Mainland now. Hawai'i is Paradise Lost.

SHIMA: You say that, but lotta haoles move to Hawai'i from the Mainland. They see something in Hawai'i they don't get on the Mainland.

LEE: Who knows why? Maybe they're running away from something.

SHIMA: Like us? We had something once. Right here in Hawai'i.

LEE: Russ, it's a different world now. A different time. What we had we lost. Even the three of us aren't as close as we were in high school.

SHIMA: Of course. We moved away. But if we had stayed in Hawai'i, the three of us would still be close.

LEE: I don't think so. You forget we were beginning to pull apart late in our senior year. We were going to take different paths in life. We learn new things, we make new friends. We don't have the same interests, so there's nothing to talk about, except the old days and that gets really old really fast.

SHIMA: In school I thought we were close to the end. Graduation night the three of us went out together.

LEE: Yeah, but we never confided in each other in school.

SHIMA: Sure we did.

LEE: No, we never told each other intimate secrets, things that touched on our vulnerability.

SHIMA: What do you want—True Confessions?

LEE: Listen, I told Ruby something the other night I never told you, Zip, or even my parents.

SHIMA: Yeah? Why Ruby?

LEE: I don't know. I think maybe if you can share an intimacy like sex with a woman, you're free to share other intimacies.

SHIMA: You told her this secret before or after you had sex?

LEE: Before.

SHIMA: Okay, you tell Ruby your innermost feelings to show how vulnerable you are. You open up to her 'cause you want her to open up—in bed.

LEE: Aeh, I was sincere.

SHIMA: I know you, Ben, you're not the sensitive, sincere type.

LEE: I've changed, man. I told Ruby the truth.

SHIMA: If you wanna play the truth game, admit you hate New York.

LEE: I love New York. I belong in the Big Apple.

SHIMA: Hell, New York doesn't give a damn about you. So, okay, I can say I love L.A., but does L.A. love me back? No.

LEE: I can't help it if you wanna be an unknown critic on a rinky-dink alternative newspaper. At least I make a lotta money.

SHIMA: Ben, I'm the best film critic in L.A. The absolute best. I know it and I'm happy and I love what I'm doing. All the money you make don't mean shit to me.

LEE: Hey, I never said you were a bad critic, did I?

SHIMA: You know, you really did change.

LEE: Of course I've changed. Man, I had to change. Survival. That's the whole point. Shima, you and me, we hadda change. Life on the Mainland is more cutthroat with the haoles. You know that. The haoles aren't gonna sit back and let you take their jobs without a fight. They don't want you taking over their turf. So I learn to deal the cards with my back to the wall. I play the game according to their rules. I talk like them, I walk like them, hell, I even think like them. And don't make like you're different from me.

SHIMA: You know what the catch is? We don't belong in New York or L.A. And we don't belong in Hawai'i anymore. We're displaced persons. Out in limbo. Neither here nor there. Sure, we try to fit in, we make believe like we're haoles, but the haoles will always look at us like we're foreigners, aliens with funny eyes and yellow skin living in their white society. I don't know if it's worth it. Pretending we're something that we're not. Maybe what we were searching for was in Hawai'i all along.

(ZIPPY returns.)

LEE: You gotta be kidding. Getting out of Hawai'i was the smartest thing I ever did. Any place is better than here. You know how small-minded people here are. How dull, how pathetic—

SHIMA: Yeah, maybe I did think that when I was in high school but not now. . . . Caught anything, Zip?

ZIPPY: Nah. Just one small one, not wort' it, so I t'rew 'um back.

LEE: See, look at Zip. Who knows what he might've become if he had gone to the Mainland like us? Right, Zip? You had the potential. Why didn't you go to the Mainland too?

ZIPPY: I liked Hawai'i, so I stayed home.

LEE: Yeah, sure, but you know what I mean. If you'd gone to the Mainland, you'd be a different person than what you are now. Would've been good for you. Broaden your horizon, that sort of thing.

ZIPPY: I did okay here.

LEE: Yeah, yeah, but, you know, this is still Hawai'i, not the Mainland, where the big boys play. Understand? You lost out by not going up with Russ and me.

ZIPPY: So I can be like you? No, t'anks.

LEE: Hey, all I'm saying is, too bad you didn't go to the Mainland with us.

ZIPPY: I neva liked da Mainland.

LEE: I know you wanted to go with us.

SHIMA: No, Ben, I remember. Zip always had the UH in mind.

LEE: No, you forget. In our junior year he was hot to go to a Mainland school. In his senior year he had to change his mind.

ZIPPY: You know you really full a shit. You go to da Mainland and you tink you hot stuff. You not betta dan me, you know dat? You not betta dan me.

LEE: Wait, wait, I never said that.

ZIPPY: Guys like you, I dunno wat happen wen you go to da Mainland. You gotta feel superior or someting. Why? Dis ain't no hick town. I dunno why guys like you tink—

LEE: What do you mean, guys like me, what the hell—

ZIPPY: You come back talking good English, ain't no big ting, brah. We all can do dat. You proud of da fact you work wit' all da haoles up dere? Make you feel like one big shot? I tell you someting, we get plenny haoles here too, or you forget dat?

LEE: All I said was you wanted to go to the Mainland too, so don't give me that crap. What the hell you getting so hot about? I'm just stating a fact: Your father got sick, so your mother said you had to stay in Hawai'i to help her and your sister.

SHIMA: You got it wrong, Ben.

LEE: No, no, dammit, don't lie to me, Zip. I know. So you couldn't go to the Mainland, so you had to stay home and help care for your father. So you didn't have the money for a Mainland school. I feel for you because I know how badly you wanted to go with us.

SHIMA: Who told you that?

LEE: His mother bumped into my mother and told her. Twenty years ago. Your mother felt sorry for you, Zip. She felt bad, but, you know. . . . You didn't want to tell us, that's up to you, wasn't my business, you wanna keep it a secret.

ZIPPY: No feel sorry for me. 'Cause you da one gotta feel sorry. And I'm gonna tell you this in good English, so you can understand. I'm glad now I didn't go to the Mainland, not if I had to turn out like you. I got a good family, lots of friends and relatives around me. I got a good life, I got more than you'll ever have. Go back to the Mainland with all your haole girlfriends and your haole lifestyle. Who cares

about that kind of life? Who wants it? Big deal, big shot. Do Hawai'i
a favor. Don't come back, we don't need you.

(*ZIPPY exits.*)

SHIMA: I don't know, I don't know.

LEE: You don't know what?

SHIMA: Why did I come back for the reunion?

LEE: That's what I said.

SHIMA: I think it's time to return to the Mainland.

LEE: When you leaving?

SHIMA: Day after tomorrow.

LEE: I'm flying out tomorrow afternoon.

SHIMA: Well, let me know if you come to L.A.

LEE: Ditto for you in New York.

SHIMA: Good.

LEE: I guess we'll never see each other in Hawai'i again.

SHIMA: You never know.

(*LEE exits in the opposite direction from ZIPPY. SHIMA addresses the
audience.*)

When I left Hawai'i, I thought I'd study on the Mainland and come
home to Honolulu to work. But then, things started twisting out of
shape. The Mainland says: "Stick around, we have jobs. You don't
have to go home again. Make a life here." And guess what? Now I've
lived longer on the Mainland than in Hawai'i. That's scary. And then
there's friendship, a fragile thing. You gotta keep working at it or it'll
evaporate when you're not looking. Or if it breaks apart, what a mess.
Sometimes, like Humpty Dumpty, you can't put it back together
again. But with a little work and patience, friendship can be patched
up. Unless friendship is only an illusion. But ours was real. It was
born in the fabulous fifties when the world shook with rock and roll.
Now life in the fifties wasn't as innocent and carefree as my nostalgic
mind likes to think. There was the Korean War, the McCarthy hear-
ings, and all that talk about atomic bombs and the threat of nuclear
annihilation. Serious baggage. But gimme a break. I wanna remember the silly and stupid escapades of three guys who grew up in a
special time, in a special place. Benjamin Gee Tim Lee, Roland Zippy
Ching, and Russell Makoto Shima. But we changed. Hawai'i changed
too. And now we're linked together only in memories. Of course,

there's also Sharon, Donna, and Ruby. But that's another story. I see all our lives as a movie, but we can't cut and splice and edit to make that perfect life, can we? But we keep trying. Maybe someday I'll get it right. And anyway you always see something new in your life every time you play it back. And I'll always remember my days in the fifties with Zippy and Ben. And I won't let them forget either. Well, see you around in L.A. Read my movie reviews—if you can find them.
(*SHIMA smiles, then exits.*)

THE END

Stew Rice, Kumu Kahua production at Kawaiahao Hall, 1987, directed by Dando Kluever. *Left to right:* Gary N. Nomura as Ben, Keith K. Kashiwada as Zippy, and Leighton Liu as Russell. PHOTO BY WENDELL MARUYAMA.

Stew Rice, Kumu Kahua production at Kawaiahao Hall, 1987, directed by Dando Kluever. The crabbing scene in Act I. *Left to right:* Gary N. Nomura as Ben, Leighton Liu as Russell, and Keith K. Kashiwada as Zippy. PHOTO BY WENDELL MARUYAMA.

Stew Rice, East West Players production at East West Players Theatre, Silver Lake, Los Angeles, 1988, directed by Dana Lee. The crabbing scene. *Left to right:* Marcus Mukai as Ben, Benjamin Lum as Zippy, and Keone Young as Russell. PHOTO COURTESY EAST WEST PLAYERS ARCHIVES.

Stew Rice, Kumu Kahua Theatre, 1995, directed by James A. Nakamoto. Ben (Michael Lee, *left*) Russell (Marcus Oshiro, *center*) and Zippy (Jason Scott Lee, *right*) get ready for a club dance as they work on decorations in Act I. PHOTO BY ERROL CHRISTIAN.

Stew Rice, Kumu Kahua Theatre, 1995, directed by James A. Nakamoto. Russell (Marcus Oshiro, *left*) Ben (Michael Lee, *center*) and Zippy (Jason Scott Lee, *right*) take a joy ride through Waikiki in Act I. PHOTO BY ERROL CHRISTIAN.

Aloha Las Vegas

Cast of Characters

WALLY FUKUDA, a retired baker, age sixty-five
JUNE FUKUDA, his daughter, a schoolteacher, age forty-one
BUTCH FUKUDA, his son, thirty-eight, a security guard
DEEDEE FUKUDA, Butch's wife, twenty-five, a secretary
ALVIN KAWABATA, fish-market owner, fifty, unmarried
GRACIE, Wally's neighbor and housekeeper, about fifty
HARRY, Wally's best friend, fifty-eight, now living in Las Vegas

TIME: 1994.

PLACE: Living room in the middle-class Liliha district of Honolulu.

SCENERY: The modest living room is neatly furnished. The kitchen is at
stage left. Kitchen door leads to the unseen backyard. At stage right
is a hallway that leads to bedrooms. There is a couch, a love seat. A
dining table with chairs is at stage right. A Japanese doll in a glass
case decorates a side table next to the couch. A half-finished jigsaw
puzzle is on the dining table.

Act One

Scene 1

*(GRACIE enters from the front door, leaves her slippers outside, and
walks barefoot in the house, as will all the other characters. She turns
on a radio cassette player, then looks out the upstage picture window. Bushes outside decorate the lower part of the window. GRACIE
takes out a cigarette from her apron pocket and lights up. A rap song
is blaring. She smokes and vacuums. The phone rings. At first she
doesn't hear it, but the phone is insistent. She stops the cleaner and
turns off the radio.)*

GRACIE: Hello. . . . No, Wally Fukuda is out. . . . Well, I dunno. He neva
say wen he coming back. . . . Okay, okay . . . yeah. Bye-bye.
*(She hangs up, then puffs on the cigarette. Offstage, the sound of a car
turning into the driveway. She quickly looks for a place to put out the
cigarette, scoots around, searching. She runs back to where she was*

133

smoking and fans the air to disperse the smoke. She hears the key in the front door and puts the cigarette in her mouth. WALLY *enters, carrying a brown bag of groceries. He smiles at* GRACIE, *but then sniffs. He walks slowly toward* GRACIE, *who edges backward with a weak smile.)*

WALLY: Gracie, you was smoking? (*She shakes her head.*)

I can smell 'um, Gracie. No can fool me. Come on. Where? (*He sticks out his hand. She meekly opens her mouth and takes out the cigarette to put in his hand.*) How many times I told you. Smoking no good.

GRACIE: I know.

WALLY: You been lighting up all dis time?

(*He drops the cigarette in a wastebasket.*)

GRACIE: Well, not all da time, not like before.

WALLY: No smoke please. No good. I like you stick around help me clean my house. If you no stay, dis house going turn into one pig house.

GRACIE: So hard not to smoke. You know, you used to smoke yourself.

WALLY: But I wen' stop. If I can, you can.

GRACIE: Yeah. You wen' stop smoking wen Kay got sick.

WALLY: One day I stop and neva smoke again. Pau.

GRACIE: Oh, by da way, somebody named Harry wen' call.

WALLY: Harry? Harry who?

GRACIE: All he said was Harry.

WALLY: Hmmm, I know t'ree Harrys. One is haole. He was haole?

GRACIE: No sound like one haole. But nowdays hard to tell.

WALLY: Da odda Harry is on da Mainland. And da last Harry dead.

GRACIE: Well, if da last Harry calling from da grave, I getting outta here.

(WALLY *takes his bag into the kitchen.* GRACIE *resumes vacuuming. Soon* WALLY *returns with a persimmon on a small dish. He goes upstage right to a small Buddhist shrine, the* butsudan. GRACIE *stops cleaning, as he goes through the ritual of lighting a candle, burning an incense stick in a small bowl, and hitting a brass bowl with a small stick three times. He holds his hands in prayer, saying "Namu Amida Butsu" three times.)*

GRACIE: I can make too?

WALLY: Oh yeah, yeah, come. Just one stick, yeah.

(GRACIE *puts an incense stick in the bowl and bows politely.* WALLY *fans out the candle flame.)*

GRACIE: How long since Kay passed away? Year and a half?

WALLY: One year, seven months.

GRACIE: Too bad, yeah. You just retired and now you two could travel and have a good time.

WALLY: Yep. Forty years as one baker. 'S enough, yeah. All da doughnuts and bear claws and eclairs, pumpkin pies . . .

GRACIE: You know wat my favorite was? Your Guava Chiffon Surprise. Hooo, da ono.

WALLY: I wen' bake my last one Friday. I not going bake nuttin' else da rest of my life.

GRACIE: I cannot orda one Guava Chiffon from you?

WALLY: Sorry, pau.

GRACIE: I tought you my friend.

WALLY: Even my relatives not going get any.

(He stands next to the dining table, looking at the jigsaw puzzle. He picks up a piece and places it in the proper spot.)

GRACIE: I dunno how you can work on dat jigsaw. Too many pieces, drive me crazy.

WALLY: Sometimes help pass da time at night.

(WALLY pushes the button on the cassette player. Frank Sinatra's "Time After Time" plays. GRACIE uses a rag to clean the coffee table.)

GRACIE: Really old song, yeah.

WALLY: Go back wen Kay and me were young . . .

GRACIE: . . . and in love.

WALLY: Our song. I told her, "I cannot sing but if I can sing, I like sing dis song to you."

(The doorbell rings. WALLY turns off the recorder and opens the door.)

HARRY: Aeh, Wally, how you doing?

WALLY: Harry! I was hoping was you. Aeh, come in, come in.

HARRY: How I look? Not bad, eh?

WALLY: Yeah, life treating you good.

HARRY: No can complain.

WALLY: Aeh, I bet you came back to live. Mainland was waste time, eh? No can beat Hawai'i.

HARRY: You kidding me? I love it up dere. I neva regret leaving Honolulu. You know me, I neva look back.

WALLY: Oh, Harry, dis is Gracie, my friend and neighbor down da street and part-time housekeepa. She really help me out plenny.

HARRY: Oh yeah? Tell me da truth, Gracie. You shacking up wit' Wally, eh?

GRACIE: No, I married.

HARRY: Oh mo' betta. You like shack up wit' me?

WALLY: No listen to dis guy, Gracie. Too smood, yeah? He live in Vegas now.

GRACIE: No wonda.

HARRY: Dey call me California Harry.

GRACIE: Okay if I call you Pupule Harry?

HARRY *(laughing):* Gracie, you so sweet. Marry me.

GRACIE: Ha! If you live in Vegas, how come dey no call you Nevada Harry?

HARRY: Because I hang out at da California Hotel in Vegas. You know da place?

GRACIE: Oh yeah, my husband and I go dere once a year, no miss, wit' my lucky frog. Good ova dere. Dey treat Hawai'i people real nice.

HARRY: 'S right. If you from Hawai'i, you get da best treatment. I live about ten minutes from da California.

WALLY: Da last time I was dere, I took Kay. She wasn't feeling too strong because of da cancer, but she wanted to go. Hit one six-hundred dollar jackpot. She was so happy wen all da coins started falling. Dat was about six months before she wen' pass away.

GRACIE: Yeah, yeah, she was telling me wen she came back. 'S right, she hit da six hundred. Oh, dat was so nice.

WALLY: Meant so much to her.

HARRY: Of course. Because she earned it. All by herself. She won. 'S da big ting. Not how much she won.

WALLY: Aeh, you like one beer?

HARRY: Nah, too early. Coffee okay.

WALLY: Yeah.

GRACIE: You folks go talk story. I make 'um.

(GRACIE exits into the kitchen.)

WALLY: How long you going stay dis time?

(The two men sit.)

HARRY: Two weeks. See some relatives.

WALLY: Everyting okay in Vegas?

HARRY: Da best, Wally, da best. Hit one twenty-five-tousand dollar jackpot. Video poker, royal flush, progressive.

WALLY: No kidding. You lucky bugga, eh.

HARRY: You know I like shoot craps, but sometimes I play da slots. Change of pace, eh. You saw my life up dere. I get up wen I like, do wat I like, nobody bodda me.

WALLY: Wen you said you going turn pro, I tought, chee, going be tough.

HARRY: Well, you gotta have discipline, you know dat. Wen I losing, I walk away from da crap table. But wen I winning, I really load up, you know, make da most of da hot hand.

WALLY: Yeah, 's one ting I get hard time doing. You gotta bring up da bets wen da hot streak is on.

HARRY: And wen da dice are cold, ice cubes, I stop. I no try force 'um. You only lose mo'.

WALLY: Control, yeah, gotta have control. No go crazy.

HARRY: Aeh, wen tings not going right, I just play twenty-five-cents video poker. 'S how I hit my jackpot. But someday I going hit da million-dollar baby.

WALLY: Me, I no mo' da kine luck. Kay used to like da slots, yeah. I told her, "Come wit' me, I show you how play craps." But no, too fast da game, she used to say. She hold her own wit' da slots, though. In fact, I bet she was ahead in winnings ova da years.

HARRY: You see how you talking? You see? Your eyes light up. You rememba da good times. And you cannot get homesick in Vegas. All you gotta do is go to da California Hotel and you always bump into people you know from Hawai'i.

WALLY: 'S true. No miss, yeah. One time we bump into Kay's cousin from Maui, and one odda time her auntie from da Big Island. Da auntie was eighty years old and she was so busy playing da slots, no mo' time for talk.

HARRY: 'S right. Aeh, old folks really love Vegas. Dey get a kick, yeah? Wen dey hit one jackpot, most a dem dey no laugh or clap or make big noise, but you look at deir faces, dey look proud. Dey wen' earn dat jackpot, man, dey work for it. Nobody had to crank da handle for dem, nobody had to help dem. Dey did 'um all by demself.

WALLY: Yeah. I can just see Kay's face now. She neva get energy to do too many tings, but she still had da strength to crank da slot handle. She could've push da spin button for make da wheels turn, but no, she wanted to pull da handle. For good luck, she said. I was hoping she hit one jackpot 'cause she was trying so hard. And wen she hit 'um, I had tears in my eyes. I was so happy for her. Yeah, Kay and me had good times in Vegas even if we neva win all da time.

HARRY: I can see her face too. She knew how to have a good time.

(GRACIE *returns with coffee mugs and a plate of cookies on a tray, placing it on the coffee table.*)

WALLY: T'anks, Gracie. Come sit down listen too.

HARRY: Wally, look. (HARRY *holds a pair of dice in his hand.*) Come on, roll 'um, see wat kine luck you get.

(WALLY *handles the dice, looking them over, then rolls them on the floor.*)

HARRY: Seven! All right!

GRACIE: Seven is good, eh?

HARRY: Oh yeah. On da come-out roll, seven or eleven is a winna.

WALLY: Here, try roll.

(GRACIE *shakes the dice with cupped hands.*)

HARRY: No, dey not let you do dat, bumbai you cheat.

GRACIE: Wat, I no cheat.

WALLY: One hand, one hand, shake 'um wit' one hand.

(*She rattles the dice with one hand.*)

HARRY: Okay, first you gotta put down one bet on da Pass Line. How much?

GRACIE: Hundred bucks!

HARRY: Hooo, da big rolla! Go 'head, betting one hundred.

(*She rolls the dice on the floor with a flourish.*)

HARRY: Two! You lose!

GRACIE: Aeh, you neva say nuttin' about losing.

HARRY: You roll two, you lose. 'S da rules. Roll 'um again. How much you betting?

GRACIE: Two hundred. I gotta get my money back.

(*She rolls with a passion.*)

HARRY: Twelve!

GRACIE: I win!

HARRY: You lose! Twelve is craps too. Loser!

GRACIE: Aeh, no fair.

WALLY: Yeah, 's wat we all say.

HARRY: No forget, seven or eleven you win.

GRACIE: And two or twelve I lose.

HARRY: Now you catching on.

WALLY: Roll 'um again and win dis time.

HARRY: No forget. How much you betting?

GRACIE: How much I lose so far?

WALLY: T'ree hundred.

GRACIE: Okay, I betting eight hundred.

HARRY: Right! Time to go to Caesars Palace!

(*GRACIE is determined. She grimaces and wiggles her hips. She rolls.*)

HARRY: T'ree!

GRACIE: I win!

HARRY: You lose! T'ree is a loser!

(*GRACIE appeals to WALLY.*)

WALLY: He not lying. Two, three, and twelve is craps, you lose.

GRACIE: Wat kine game dis? Junk. Only two, three, and twelve come out.
Dis dice must be crooked.

(*She examines the dice carefully.*)

HARRY: You just on one losing streak. You going win. Roll 'um, baby,
roll 'um.

GRACIE: Okay, betting . . . one tousand!

HARRY: All right, go for it!

(*She rolls.*)

WALLY: Four.

GRACIE: I win?

WALLY: No, now you gotta roll da numba four again, den you win.

GRACIE: Good.

HARRY: But—

GRACIE: Wat but, I no like but!

HARRY: But now you gotta roll da four before you roll da seven. If you
get da seven before you get da four, you lose.

GRACIE: I tought if I roll seven I win.

HARRY: 'S only on da come-out roll.

WALLY: See, da point of da game is to roll four, five, six, eight, nine, or ten. Wen you roll one of dese numbas, you gotta roll again and hit da same numba. See, you wen' roll da four, right? Now you roll da four again, you win. But if you roll seven, you lose.

HARRY: 'S only wen you no mo' numba to roll, wat dey call da come-out roll, den you lose two, three, or twelve and you win wit' seven or eleven.

GRACIE: Wait, wait, I getting dizzy. Humbug, eh, dis game.

HARRY: Easy once you know all da rules. Roll 'um, Gracie.

(GRACIE *is about to roll dramatically.*)

WALLY: Wait!

(*She spins around in a wild gyration and falls on her butt.*)

GRACIE: Wassamatta!

WALLY: You gotta back up your Pass Line bet wit' double odds.

HARRY: Yeah, yeah, yeah, no forget da odds. Put two tousand behind da bet. Always take da double odds.

GRACIE: If you say so.

WALLY: Now you t'ree tousand riding on da roll.

HARRY: Dis wahine tough, eh, Wally? Gracie, you tough.

(*She flexes her muscles.*)

WALLY: Okay, roll dat four.

(*She rolls.*)

HARRY: Eight.

GRACIE: I win.

WALLY: No, no. How can?

GRACIE (*pointing*): Das da four. And das da four.

HARRY: Equals eight. But eight no harm. In fact, if you roll six, eight, five, nine, ten, 's good, 'cause da odda bettors get money on dose odda numbas. If you roll dose numbas ova and ova, dey love you.

GRACIE: Dey no like I roll da four?

HARRY: Dey like dat too.

GRACIE: Dey gotta make up deir mind, eh. Here comes da four.

(*She rolls again.*)

HARRY: T'ree and one . . . four, winna!

(GRACIE *dances and whoops it up.*)

WALLY: Lessee, you win tousand for da Pass Line bet, double for da odds bet, 's four tousand. All togedda you get eight tousand.

GRACIE: All right, all right!

HARRY: How much you like bet now?

GRACIE: Bet 'um all, I not chicken shit, bet 'um all.

WALLY: Wow, wait, no limit on da crap table. We mean business.

HARRY: Let da lady roll!

(GRACIE *resumes her comical ritual. Then she rolls.*)

HARRY: Aaaaaggghhh! Ten!

GRACIE: Wat?

HARRY: You sure make it hard, Gracie.

GRACIE: Why?

WALLY: Ten is a hard numba to roll.

GRACIE: I like ten. Good even numba. Five and five is ten.

WALLY: Okay. Confidence, 's good. Go for da hard way, five and five.

HARRY: Back up wit' da odds, no forget.

GRACIE: Gimme everyting on da odds.

WALLY: 'S sixteen tousand behind da line.

GRACIE: I no mo' sixteen tousand.

HARRY: No sweat. I back you up, sista. I loan you sixteen tousand. I believe in you. I believe.

WALLY: Now you get eight tousand on da Pass Line and sixteen tousand behind, 's twenty-four tousand riding on da ten.

GRACIE: Wait, wait, I need one cigarette.

WALLY: No mo' time smoke, you holding up da game.

GRACIE: Look my hand (*it's trembling*), too much pressure.

WALLY: You can do it, Gracie. I know you, you can do it. Just go for broke!

HARRY: Come on, Gracie, shake dem bones.

WALLY: You tough, Gracie, da Iron Buttafly, 's you. Work your hips. Hang loose. Cool head main ting.

(GRACIE *nods knowingly. She calms down, then goes through her ritual. Finally, for sheer coolness, she flips the dice behind her back.*)

HARRY: Aaaaaahhhhhh . . . five . . . four!

(GRACIE *screams and falls near the dice.*)

GRACIE: You see wat happen? I had one five and one mo' five was turning up but wen' hit dis dirt here and turn up four. 'S wat I get, I neva vacuum dis spot good.

WALLY: 'S okay. Nine is no harm. You can still get da ten.

GRACIE: Yeah, yeah. You betting wit' me, Wally? I hot, I hot.

WALLY: I backing you up all da way.

HARRY: Aeh, I get so much confidence in you, I going bet da limit on da hard way ten—five and five.

GRACIE: Okay, baby, okay. You want da five and five, you got it!
(She rolls.)

WALLY: Five and five! Hard way ten!
(GRACIE whoops and high-fives WALLY and HARRY.)

GRACIE: How much I win?

WALLY: Eight tousand for da Pass bet, t'irty-two tousand for da odds bet, all togedda you get sixty-four tousand dollars.

GRACIE: Sixty-four tousand! Wait till I tell my husband.

HARRY: Next time you come to Vegas, you gotta come see me and we hit da crap table togedda. We can break 'um, Gracie, you and me, we can break 'um.

GRACIE: Okay, next time for sure. Now I know why da crap table so full wit' people screaming and cheering.

WALLY: 'S da best time. Good fun and you make lotta money.

GRACIE: Yeah, yeah, I see. Okay, I ready, I ready. Look out, everybody, gimme room, I betting da whole sixty-four tousand dollars.

WALLY: No, you pupule or wat?

GRACIE: I like bet da whole sixty-four tousand.

WALLY: Wat if you lose?

HARRY: It's discipline, discipline. You walk away a winna. No let da casino win your money back. One guy once won one million dollars at da crap table at da Horseshoe in 1991. But da dumb ass wen' lose 'um all back. Yeah! All da one million. Was in newspaper. So you take da sixty-four tousand wit' you and be happy.

GRACIE: But no can buy nuttin' wit' dis sixty-four tousand. 'S why hard. I go from one big rolla back to housekeepa just li'dat *(snaps her fingers)*. Coffee cold. You like fresh one?

HARRY: No, cold betta for da stomach.
(GRACIE goes off.)
Wally, we gotta hit da crap table togedda. Man, I tell you, I need you standing right next to me for good luck.

WALLY: Maybe someday.
(GRACIE returns with a Dust Buster and makes a point of vacuuming the spot where the dice were rolled earlier.)

GRACIE: Now okay.

(She goes into the kitchen.)

HARRY: Wally, listen to dis. Now just listen, okay? Why you no move to Vegas like me?

WALLY: Live in Vegas?

HARRY: Yeah, why not? Aeh, lodda Hawai'i people moving to Vegas. Da promised land, Wally, da promised land.

WALLY: Wat I going do dere?

HARRY: Wat you mean, you do wat I do. Gamble, live da good life. Play some golf, no worries, no cares in da world.

WALLY: For you maybe, you not married.

HARRY: Well, you know, you too.

WALLY: Hmmm, I neva tought of dat. I still feel like I married to Kay.

HARRY: You free to do wateva you like. Go any place you can imagine. Nobody bodda you.

WALLY: Well, I get June and Butch.

HARRY: Yeah but dey grown up already.

GRACIE *(from kitchen entrance):* Nice kids. I wish was mine. I no mo' kids. Only my husband Teddy and my dog Moe Lepo.

WALLY: You need money live in Vegas.

HARRY: Aeh, look at dis house. You can get, I figga, minimum six hundred tousand. And no forget, you qualify for da two-hundred-fifty-tousand tax-free exemption on da sale. In Vegas right now, in Nort' Las Vegas where I live, you can buy one brand-new four-bedroom house for one hundred twenty tousand dollars.

GRACIE: 'S all? Cheap.

WALLY: Yeah, sounds good.

HARRY: Oh real nice da house. 'S why lodda Hawai'i people moving to Vegas. Good desert climate. Food is cheap.

GRACIE: Dis one girl I know. She used to work as one hairdressa. Den she wen' move to Vegas. She selling real estate now. All her beauty-shop clients, she selling Vegas property to dem now. Akamai.

HARRY: Yeah, she smart. Aeh, it's a mass exodus to Vegas. Lodda people in Hawai'i house-rich and cash-poor. So you sell your equity-rich house here and buy one nice new house in Vegas for one-fifth da price and you bank da rest of da money. No can beat dat.

WALLY: Bumbai I lose all my money gambling.

HARRY: Not you. You get control.

GRACIE: Somebody else.

WALLY: Wat?

GRACIE: Da Kukona family. Dey bought one condo so da daughta get one place to stay wen she attend UNLV. And wen dey visit Vegas, dey stay wit' da daughta.

HARRY: Wally, people starting a new life in Vegas. And why not? You bust your ass all dese years making a living, sending da kids to school, taking care of da old folks, now you can relax and get some fun, enjoy life.

WALLY: I guess so.

HARRY: Yeah. Aeh, we go out dinna dis week. We can talk some mo'.

WALLY: Okay sure. You like I call you?

HARRY: No, I get in touch wit' you. I gotta see some odda people. I stay at da Halekulani. Gracie, nice meeting you. No forget, we hit da crap table togedda next time.

GRACIE: Yeah and I bringing my sixty four tousand wit' me.

WALLY: See you, eh. Good you came visit.

HARRY: Okay, bye.

(*HARRY leaves.*)

WALLY: Wat you tink, Gracie. Me live in Vegas.

GRACIE: I cannot picture you living in one desert. 'S wat Vegas is, one desert. You one Hawai'i boy. No can beat da aloha spirit here.

WALLY: Yeah, you right. And Vegas starting to get smog too, you know.

GRACIE: Oh yeah?

WALLY: Sure. Hawai'i get clean, fresh air. Beautiful beaches. You know how much I like da beach. And da last time I was in Vegas I neva see one beach. Anyway, I cannot leave Butch and June behind, especially June. She not married, so I gotta watch ova her.

GRACIE: 'S right. Your only daughta, afta all.

WALLY: Yup. If I neva get kids, well den, 's someting else.

(*WALLY is deep in thought as lights fade slowly to black.*)

Scene 2

(*Lights up. It is a couple of days later. WALLY is alseep on the couch with a blanket completely covering him. GRACIE enters through the front door, heads toward the kitchen. She sees a mess and shakes her head. She throws some rubbish into a wastebasket, sneezes, and grabs a tissue from the coffee table.* WALLY *doesn't move under the blanket.* GRACIE *walks to the hallway entrance to listen for* WALLY. *Then she returns and plops down on the couch.* WALLY *grunts loudly, and* GRACIE *jumps up with a scream. He emerges from under the blanket.)*

WALLY: Wat was dat? Felt like someting wen' sit on me.

GRACIE: Oh, you was dreaming.

WALLY: I guess so. Musta been one elephant.

GRACIE: Aeh, aeh!

WALLY: Wat?

GRACIE: Neva mind. How come you sleeping on da couch?

WALLY: I been sleeping on da couch long time now.

GRACIE: How long?

WALLY: Eva since Kay wen' pass away.

GRACIE: Why? No good li'dat.

WALLY: Cannot help. Too hard sleep in da bedroom.

GRACIE: Oh, too bad, no.

WALLY: I like da couch. Comfortable.

GRACIE: Why you still sleeping?

WALLY: I was out late wit' Harry last night.

GRACIE: Where you guys went?

WALLY: All ova. Dinna at Wisteria. Harry miss da local soul food. Den we wen' see da Frank DeLima show. Was good. And last, we wen' hit da karaoke bar across da street from A'ala Park, by da skating rink.

GRACIE: Busy night, eh. Old futs like you guys can still have fun, yeah?

WALLY: Harry is one good fun guy.

GRACIE: You like I cook breakfast for you?

(WALLY folds the blanket neatly.)

WALLY: I make 'um myself. Only easy fry Spam and eggs.

GRACIE: I wish Teddy was mo' like you. He like tings like Eggs Benedict. I tell 'um, you going eat Eggs Gracie and no squawk, two eggs sunny-side down and da yolk all broke up.

(JUNE enters at the front door.)

JUNE: Hi, Gracie. Daddy, you still in your pajamas?

WALLY: I just woke up.

JUNE: That's not like you. What time did you sleep?

WALLY: T'ree o'clock.

JUNE: What were you doing up so late?

WALLY: Wat, no can . . . no can . . . work on my puzzle? You see here, not so easy. Suppose to be one t'ree-ring circus.

JUNE: Daddy, if you're gonna stay up late working on the puzzle, you better stop. Not good for you.

WALLY: Aeh, little bit kapakahi, eh. Who da parent and who da child around here? I suppose to tell you dat.

JUNE: You know I'm always in bed by ten-thirty.

WALLY: Well, 's da trouble. Maybe you should go out and have a good time, go to one karaoke bar like m-m-m-m Gracie. You stay home too much. Find one nice boyfriend and go out and laugh and drink and—

JUNE: I don't drink, you know that. And we went over this long time ago. I'm forty-one years old. I'm gonna be like Auntie Kiku, an old maid.

(JUNE goes into the kitchen with a small box she brought.)

GRACIE: You get fast mout', eh. I like da way you wen' squeeze oudda dat.

WALLY: Aeh, no good if she know her faddah was out at da bar drinking till closing time.

JUNE *(from kitchen)*: Daddy, you ate breakfast yet?

WALLY: No.

JUNE: You want me to make toast for you?

WALLY: 'S all she know how make. She neva learn how cook.

JUNE: Daddy!

WALLY: Make me miso soup.

JUNE: I don't know how.

WALLY: See.

GRACIE: Why Kay neva teach her?

WALLY: June neva like learn.

GRACIE: How she eat now?

WALLY: Frozen dinnas. Go out eat. You know, nowdays no need cook.

(JUNE returns with a small dish of manju which she puts at the shrine. She doesn't go through the ritual, just bows with palms together.)

JUNE: I brought some manju but don't eat now. Eat after lunch or dinner right after the meal.

WALLY: Who said dat?

JUNE: Nutritionists.

WALLY: Who dat?

JUNE: People who know what and how you should eat.

WALLY: Sound like busybodies.

JUNE: Behave now. Gracie, try the manju. Come.

> (*They go into the kitchen.*)

WALLY: Aeh, how come Gracie can eat now?

GRACIE: 'Cause I not one old fut like you.

WALLY: I know I just retired, but I no feel old.

JUNE: You know why.

WALLY: No, I dunno why. If I know why, I no ask. (*To himself.*) You know wat she talking about? No ask me, I just live here.

JUNE: Daddy, go change.

WALLY: Why? I like stay in my pajamas. Hugh Hefner stay in his pajamas all day.

JUNE: You're not Hugh Hefner, thank goodness.

GRACIE: Yeah, if you Hugh Hefner, I gotta be da Playboy bunny.

JUNE: I'm going jogging. Let's go. You can just walk.

WALLY: If I like walk, I can walk in da house.

JUNE: Not the same. Get some fresh air, sweat a little. You don't do anything since Mama got sick.

WALLY: Aeh, how come you eating one manju too?

JUNE: Well, I'm gonna exercise from now, so it's okay.

WALLY: You mean, if I go exercise wit' you, I can eat one too?

JUNE: Well . . .

WALLY: Aeh, 's how you teach your students? Do as I say, not as I do.

JUNE: Okay, you can eat one. Only one.

> (WALLY *quickly slips into the kitchen and returns eating a manju.*)

JUNE: I was thinking, since you're retired now, maybe you have time to pack up Mama's clothes to give away.

WALLY: No need.

JUNE: Give you more room in the closet. And some people can use her clothes.

WALLY: Nah, nah, nah.

JUNE: You want me to do it? I can—

WALLY: I get enough room, neva mind.

JUNE: Okay, go change your clothes then. I'll wait for you.

WALLY: No need change clothes. I change my mind instead. I not going.

JUNE: You promised.

WALLY: So I wen' lie. Wen guys reach sixty-five, dey can lie all dey like. Anyway, I get lodda tings to do.

JUNE: Like what?

WALLY: Like . . . too many to mention. And neva mind me. About time you get married. I cannot wait foreva. Someday I going be gone.

JUNE: Don't talk like that. Don't think about dying.

WALLY: I no mean dat. I just saying someday I might be gone from dis house. 'S why I like you get married so I don't have to worry about you. I like you be happy.

JUNE: I don't have to be married to be happy. I'm very busy without a man in my life. You're the man in my life, that's enough.

WALLY: No, you deserve one good husband who can take care of you da rest of your life. 'S all I get to say. Bye-bye.

(He exits into hallway.)

JUNE: He must've gotten up on the wrong side of the bed.

GRACIE: Wrong side of da couch.

JUNE: Wat?

GRACIE: He just one big grouch.

JUNE: Well, if he's not coming, I might as well go. Bye.

GRACIE: Bye-bye.

(JUNE exits. WALLY reenters, still in his pajamas.)

WALLY: Wat you tink? About time June get married, yeah?

GRACIE: Well, if she like get married.

WALLY: About time, about time.

GRACIE: Why all of a sudden you like she get da ring on da finga?

WALLY: Somebody gotta take care of her if I no stay around.

GRACIE: I hate to say dis, but if wahine no marry by forty-one, well, hard luck case, yeah.

WALLY: I dunno why June neva get married. She had chance. Some boys liked her. But she go out wit' dem one, two times, den pau. Same old story every time.

GRACIE: Well, she's a schoolteacha. She get her rules and you know she always like you follow da rules, just like her students. I can see where she going be da boss in da house and not da husband. So she gotta find somebody who like da wife be da boss.

WALLY: You know one guy li'dat for June?

GRACIE: Chee, all da good ones li'dat married already. Wahine not dumb, you know. Dey jump quick on da kine easy meat.

WALLY: Yeah, 's da trouble. 'S wat June get, wait so long. She was too picky from way back. Dis boy get too many pimples. So I said, "No judge one boy by his pimples. You dunno wat stay behind da pimples." Dat boy get crooked teet'. I said, "Crooked teet' no problem. Just tell him no smile. At least his face not crooked." Dis guy bolohead. So I said, "You save money. No need buy hair oil for him." Dat boy too fat. I said, "Dat fat boy going always be fait'ful to you 'cause no odda wahine going like one big bamboola like him." I tink I wen' little bit too far wen I said dat. But no can please June. You know how long she was living wit' Kay and me? Too long.

GRACIE: In a way, I no blame her. Was nice for her living wit' one good Daddy and good Mommy. Wat mo' can one child ask for? Even one grown-up child like June.

WALLY: Yeah but da time came wen she hadda move out for her own sake. Kay and me, we wen' talk it ova and we tought betta let her get her own place, so she can get boyfriends to come ova visit her.

GRACIE: And shack up.

WALLY: No, not dat. I like she get married.

GRACIE: 'S da way you get married nowdays. First you gotta hook 'um, den you live togedda and put da ring in da nose and drag da poor guy around.

WALLY: Not June.

GRACIE: 'S da way I wen' bag my Teddy. He was like one blue marlin. Took me long time reel him in.

WALLY: June hate fishing.

GRACIE: Fishing? Wait. I know one guy, Kawabata. Single guy. How come I wen' forget him? Oh, I know why. 'Cause he's one easy guy to forget. But he's a good man. I remema him now 'cause he own one fish market.

WALLY: 'S good. June like fish. She always telling me I gotta eat mo' fish. Wait, he divorce wit' five kids?

GRACIE: Dis guy neva been married.

WALLY: How old?

GRACIE: Fifty.

WALLY: Fifty? He not mahu?

GRACIE: No, he live at home wit' his folks, watch ova dem. Da Kawabata old lady like da son get married befo' she ma-ke.

WALLY: I can meet da guy first?

GRACIE: Yeah, I can bring him ova.

WALLY: I know. Bring him Saturday night. All da family going be ova. Where his fish market?

GRACIE: Pearl City. Good steady business.

WALLY: Sure, people gotta eat. People always eat fish. Fish good for you. 'S wat June always says.

(*Lights fade to black.*)

Scene 3

(*Lights up. Early evening.* WALLY *enters from bedroom area and heads for the kitchen. The doorbell rings and he turns to open the door.* GRACIE *and* ALVIN KAWABATA *enter.*)

WALLY: Yeah, hi, hi, come in.

GRACIE: Wally, dis is Alvin Kawabata.

WALLY: Good, good, hi.

ALVIN: Fine, t'anks.

WALLY: Oh. Yeah, yeah, okay.

ALVIN: I brought some opihi.

WALLY: Opihi. Chee, hard to get opihi nowdays. T'anks, eh.

ALVIN: I get my own source. Secret. I cannot tell you who.

WALLY: Das okay.

GRACIE: You guys go sit down talk story. I can help in da kitchen.

(*She enters the kitchen.*)

WALLY: So, ah, Gracie told you I get one daughta.

(ALVIN *nods shyly.*)

Well, I'm her faddah so I can say she one nice girl but . . . Gracie, wat you tink of June?

GRACIE: Nice girl.

WALLY: See. So, anyway. You looking for one wife?

ALVIN: Well . . . ah, ah . . .

WALLY: I hear your muddah like you settle down. Bet you get lodda girl-friends, eh?

ALVIN: No.

WALLY: So, Alvin. Wat your friends call you?

ALVIN: I no mo' too many friends.

WALLY: Some people call you, wat, Al?

ALVIN: No, just Alvin.

WALLY: You no mo' nickname?

ALVIN: Not now. Wen I was young, some kids used to call me Kawabata Hanabata.

WALLY: Oh yeah? Kawabata Hanabata.

ALVIN: Rhyme 's why.

WALLY: Yeah, yeah.

ALVIN: I rememba telling my faddah, why our name was not Kawasaki or Kawamura or—

WALLY: Kawahara.

ALVIN: Yeah.

WALLY: 'S why hard, yeah. But Alvin . . . Alvin is da name of one chipmunk. Al . . . vin, Al . . . vin. Vin. Vin. Vinny. Aeh, Vinny Kawabata. I can call you Vinny?

ALVIN: Vinny? 'S not one Italian name?

WALLY: Italian, Japanese, wat da diff'rence. Vinny Kawabata sound good.

ALVIN: Vinny. I dunno.

WALLY: Alvin is okay, no get me wrong. But Vinny is mo' macho. Aeh, Vinny! Vinny baby! Give me five, Vinny! Try walk around, go, walk. (ALVIN *takes some hesitant steps.*) 'S him, Vinny Kawabata. Aeh, Vinny, shaka, man, shaka! (ALVIN *bops up and down.*) Aeh, Vinny, all da wahines asking for you.

GRACIE: Aeh, Vinny, you make my skin hot!

WALLY: You see! Vinny, Vinny, you get da moves now!
(ALVIN *takes small, jerky steps.*)

ALVIN: You get bat'room?

WALLY: Yeah, I get two bat'rooms, t'ree bedrooms.

ALVIN: I gotta go.

WALLY: Oh, oh. Right t'rough dere and first door on da left.
(ALVIN *exits.*)

GRACIE: Well, wat you tink?

WALLY: I tink he get weak bladda.

GRACIE: Good match for June, eh?
(*She brings over a bowl of potato chips, puts it on the coffee table.*)

WALLY: I dunno if she like fish dat much.

GRACIE: Da mo' you know Alvin, I mean Vinny, da betta you like him. June would like Vinny. Give 'um chance, Wally.

(*Front door opens and* JUNE *enters.*)

JUNE: Hi, everybody. I brought M&M candies and poi.

(*She goes into the kitchen.*)

WALLY: Make me one poi cocktail.

JUNE: Not now, Daddy, going spoil your appetite.

WALLY: I wen' invite one friend for dinna.

JUNE: Who?

WALLY: You neva meet him before. He stay in da bat'room now.

(JUNE *comes out with a small bowl of* M&M *candies.*)

JUNE: Help yourself, Gracie. Daddy, afta dinna you can have some M&Ms.

(ALVIN *peeks out from upstage. He tries beckoning to* WALLY. JUNE *spots him.*)

JUNE: Somebody wants you, I think.

(WALLY *sees* ALVIN, *who meekly motions for him to come.*)

WALLY (*to women*): Try wait.

(*He steps over to* ALVIN, *listens and nods, then returns.*)

WALLY: Ah, 's Vinny Kawabata ova dere. Before he come ova, he like everybody know dat da bat'room faucet wen' crazy and he neva do wat look like he did. Okay, Vinny, come. (ALVIN *walks over sheepishly. The crotch area of his pants is dark and wet.*) Vinny, dis is my daughta June.

JUNE: Hello.

ALVIN: Fine, t'anks.

WALLY: Come sit here.

(*He sits* ALVIN *on the couch with* JUNE.)

GRACIE: Help yourself to da candy and chips.

WALLY: June, you guys talk. I gotta show Gracie someting.

GRACIE: Wat?

WALLY: Outside, come, I—

GRACIE: I busy in da kitchen.

WALLY: Important, outside da front door. Hurry up.

(*They exit.* ALVIN *helps himself to the chips. Munch, munch.*)

JUNE: I thought I knew all my father's friends, but I guess not. Where did you two meet?

ALVIN: Oh, ah, he didn't tell you?

JUNE: No.

ALVIN: Well, long time ago. Your faddah like basketball?

JUNE: No, his favorite is baseball.

ALVIN: Baseball, yeah, me too. Years ago wen I was one kid, I met your faddah.

JUNE: Oh, I know. He used to go to Honolulu Stadium back in the old days and see the local teams play.

ALVIN: He did? I mean, yeah, just like me. I used to go see dem play every weekend. And your faddah, just last year I met him again.

JUNE: He remembered you?

ALVIN: Yeah, he get good memory. He said he could neva forget me because of my nickname, Kawabata Hanabata.

(WALLY *and* GRACIE *peer in through the picture window.*)

JUNE: What? My father called you that?

ALVIN: Oh no, all da kids used to call me dat. In fact, your faddah gave me da nickname Vinny so nobody would tease me. Yeah, yeah, yeah.

(*He sighs in relief and grabs more chips.* JUNE *eyes him eating.*)

JUNE: So, what do you do?

ALVIN (*munching*): I own one fish market.

JUNE: That's nice.

ALVIN: And I live wit' my folks. Or dey live wit' me, wateva.

JUNE: I know. I used to live with my parents a while back. Now I live in a condo.

ALVIN: Oh yeah? Where?

JUNE: Kukui Plaza. (*Now he eats some* M&Ms, *pops them in one at a time.*) Your mother must feed you well.

ALVIN: Yeah, she's a good cook.

JUNE: What does she cook?

ALVIN: Fried chicken, her pineapple spareribs is good, corned beef and cabbage . . .

JUNE: The corned beef has a lot of fat, right?

ALVIN: Yeah, 's da best kine. Da fatty part taste da most ono.

JUNE: You don't eat fish?

ALVIN: My folks like 'um, but I hate fish.

JUNE: Fish is good for your diet. You should eat fish at least once a week.

ALVIN: But I see so many dead fish every day, I radda eat steaks and roast pork.

JUNE: Too much of that food is bad for you. You're just like my father. *(ALVIN reaches for more chips. Instinctively JUNE slaps his hand.)* Oh I'm sorry. Go eat. I didn't mean—

ALVIN: Bad for me, yeah. I betta stop.

JUNE: No, no, eat.

(She puts the bowl of chips on his lap. WALLY and GRACIE are still watching when BUTCH and DEEDEE join them. WALLY is startled, and they all withdraw.)

ALVIN: I betta save room for dinna. Wat do you do, your job?

JUNE: Schoolteacher. Maemae Elementary.

ALVIN: Oh yeah? I went to elementary school once.

(BUTCH, DEEDEE, GRACIE, and WALLY enter. BUTCH wears a security guard uniform.)

BUTCH: Hi, hi, hi.

DEEDEE: We not late, I hope.

JUNE: You came just in time.

WALLY: Butch, dis my friend, Vinny Kawabata. Vinny, my son Butch and his beautiful wife DeeDee.

BUTCH: Howzit. *(He gives ALVIN the local handshake, only ALVIN doesn't know it and fumbles around.)* Aeh, all dose chips for you?

ALVIN: Oh no, no, here.

(JUNE takes the bowl and puts it on the table. BUTCH helps himself.)

BUTCH: Time for eat or wat?

DEEDEE: We just came. Sit down and talk little while.

BUTCH: Daddy, Forty-niners versus Rams, plus ten Rams.

WALLY: Chee, gotta go wit' da Rams, eh, dey can beat da spread.

BUTCH: I dunno, Rams good for nuttin'. Wat for dinna?

WALLY: Oxtail stew.

BUTCH *(to ALVIN)*: Aeh, da damn stew is onolicious. Time for chow down, eh?

GRACIE: Everyting not ready yet.

WALLY: Relax, Butch, I like you get to know Vinny betta.

BUTCH: Wat for? He get someting I like?

DEEDEE: Butch!

BUTCH: Aeh, just joking, Vinny.

WALLY: He wen' bring some opihi.

BUTCH: No kidding. Where you got 'um from?

ALVIN: I cannot tell you. Secret.

BUTCH: Oh yeah? Vinny, if I like you tell me, I can get 'um oudda you. Security guards, you know, we get our ways. I get you in one small room wit' one light bulb ova your head and I question you till I squeeze 'um oudda you like toot'paste from one tube.

ALVIN: Okay, okay, I tell you.

JUNE: No, don't. Butch is just practicing his intimidation technique.

BUTCH: C'mon, June, you always spoiling my fun. I had him on da ropes.

WALLY: I neva tell you, Butch is one security guard.

BUTCH: Good one too.

WALLY: Vinny own one fish market.

BUTCH: Yeah? You get one security system hooked up in your business?

ALVIN: No, only one small place.

BUTCH: No matta, nowdays you gotta protect yourself. Times are hard, people desperate. Guard yourself at all times.

(BUTCH moves as if he's drawing a revolver and flashes his finger gun at ALVIN, who promptly raises his arms. GRACIE brings a beer for BUTCH.)

GRACIE: Butch, you t'irsty, eh?

BUTCH: Aeh, t'anks, Gracie.

(He takes good gulps of the beer.)

GRACIE: Vinny, you neva read about Butch? Couple a years ago, he arrested dese two robbas all by himself. Da story was in da *Advertisa* and *Star-Bulletin*.

DEEDEE: His picture too.

BUTCH: Was nuttin'. Dose two guys neva had a chance. I slam one guy in da head wit' my flashlight and kick da odda guy in balls. Down, man, dey wen' down. One, two. Knockout, blackout.

WALLY: Das wen DeeDee and Butch wen' meet. She was one secretary dere.

BUTCH: Yeah, I wen' spark her and I said, right dere, 's da girl for me. Right, baby?

DEEDEE: Yeah, for me too.

BUTCH: I mean, I knew right away. You know? You eva had dat feeling?

ALVIN: No.

BUTCH: Well, aeh, you get time yet. No give up hope. Going come for you someday.

ALVIN: I hope so.

GRACIE: Well, I tink we can eat now.

BUTCH: Okay, good, I going whack 'um, man.

WALLY: Try wait. I like tell all of you someting first.

BUTCH: Aeh, Daddy, no can wait till afta we eat? Da kaukau going get cold and den wat?

WALLY: I know, but dis is important.

ALVIN: Ah, I betta go den.

WALLY: No, stay, stay.

ALVIN: I can wait in da bat'room.

WALLY: You betta not. Bumbai you wet your pants again.

(BUTCH eyes ALVIN suspiciously.)

ALVIN *(standing):* Maybe betta if—

(BUTCH holds him down with one hand.)

BUTCH: No sweat, brah, easy, easy, cool down.

WALLY: Okay den. Now I was tinking real hard about dis. You see, I made sixty-five, so I old enough to figga out wat is good and wat is bad. But in dis case, I dunno da real answer yet. But anyway das why I like tell you wat on my mind.

(There is a pause as everyone waits for WALLY to continue. But he doesn't.)

JUNE: Daddy, what? What do you want to say?

WALLY: Huh? Well, not so easy to, you know, explain all dis. Because, you know, get mo' dan one side, get maybe two or t'ree sides and so I—

JUNE: Daddy!

WALLY: Wat you tink if I move?

JUNE: Move? Move what?

WALLY: Move from dis house.

BUTCH: Maybe you like move, but where you can go? Every place still expensive on Oahu. And outside islands not cheap too.

JUNE: This Liliha area is good for you. You know all the neighbors. Everything is so convenient. Life is good here.

WALLY: 'S true. But wat you tink about me moving to Vegas?

BUTCH: Las Vegas?

JUNE: You cannot live in Las Vegas.

WALLY: I neva said I going, but lodda Hawaiʻi people moving to Vegas. Right, Butch?

BUTCH: Oh yeah, I know some guys. Aeh, get about forty retired police officers living dere now.

WALLY: See? And couples, families moving dere too. Ask Gracie.

GRACIE: Wat? No ask me nuttin'.

WALLY: Tell dem about your hairdressa.

GRACIE: She not my hairdressa anymore.

WALLY: Because she wen' move to Vegas. And she doing good now as one real estate lady.

GRACIE: 'S wat I hear.

WALLY: See? So das why I was tinking, maybe, wat if I move to Vegas, I wonda wat would happen.

JUNE: No, Daddy, absolutely no. Get that idea from your head right now.

WALLY: Yeah, I guess you right. But I was tinking even Butch and DeeDee could go too.

BUTCH: Me and Dee?

WALLY: Yeah. You can find one security guard job up dere real easy. Maybe in one a da casinos. And DeeDee, da place you work wen' lay you off, so you free to go. Hard to find jobs in Hawaiʻi anyway. Wat if you can be like Gracie's friend and learn real estate too. Hawaiʻi people like buy Vegas property for investment. Lodda dat going around.

DEEDEE: But I would have to go to real estate school or something.

WALLY: No problem for you, you get education. And you get plenny friends too. I bet deir families like invest in Vegas.

BUTCH: Wat you tink, Vinny?

ALVIN: I dunno, I just own one fish market.

BUTCH: You eva go to Vegas?

ALVIN: Once a year I take da old folks. Dey like Vegas.

WALLY: Everybody like Vegas.

JUNE: Not me.

WALLY: June, you come up too.

JUNE: I hate Vegas. Daddy, you cannot go. What about Mama?

WALLY: Mama always liked going to Vegas.

JUNE: But not to live. She loved Hawai'i. She'd never have left Hawai'i for good.

WALLY: Butch, wat you tink? You ready to go?

BUTCH: Chee, I wonda. I guess I can get one good security guard job up dere. I get good record. How you feel, Dee?

DEEDEE: I don't wanna leave my parents behind.

BUTCH: Aeh, not going be li'dat. You get two bruddahs and one sista, so dat part no need worry.

DEEDEE: Wat? You made up your mind already.

BUTCH: No, but gotta tink, eh. Maybe my faddah get one good idea. Gotta talk about it.

DEEDEE: We can talk wen we get home.

WALLY: Try listen. You know my good friend Harry visiting from Vegas. And he said, brand-new four-bedroom house in North Las Vegas— one hundred twenty tousand dollars. All da appliances, ready to move in. Only hundred twenty tousand dollars.

BUTCH: Wat you tink, cheap, yeah?

ALVIN: I dunno. Ask me da price of ulua.

JUNE: What about the crime in Vegas? I read that per capita they have more crime in Vegas than in any other city in the country. What do you think about that, Butch?

BUTCH: Aeh, dat means I can find one security job easier up dere.

JUNE: Vegas is not up there. Up there, like you're talking about heaven or something. Vegas is down there, Vegas is hell. Gambling, prostitution, crooks. Daddy, people lose everything in Vegas. They lose their home gambling there. You know the Murata man. He sold his gas station, his house, and moved to Vegas. Then he lost it all.

WALLY: Yeah, da poor guy. I hear he dealing Twenty-One at El Cortez now. But he neva get control, 's why. You gotta have control.

JUNE: And you have control?

WALLY: Of course.

BUTCH: Aeh, you dunno 'cause you neva dere, but Daddy get control. He's good. You good, Daddy, I tell you dat right now.

JUNE: All I know is that it's a crazy idea.

BUTCH: Aeh, but if you really tink about it, not so—

DEEDEE: Butch, will you shut up?

BUTCH: Wat? Aeh, I just talking, wassamatta wit' dat, no can talk?

DEEDEE: Wat about wat I tink?

BUTCH: You can talk, you get mout', nobody stopping you.

DEEDEE: Shut up, you. I going home.

(She starts for the door.)

BUTCH: Yeah, just try. I get da key.

DEEDEE: No, stupid. I drove ova.

BUTCH: Oh yeah.

WALLY: DeeDee, wait.

DEEDEE: I gotta go. Dis dumb bugga get me so mad.

(She exits.)

BUTCH: Aeh, Dee, no make ass li'dat! Wat I said? See wat I go t'rough, Daddy. No can talk wit' her. But, you know, about Vegas—if you like, I can call dese guys in Vegas and ask dem to look around for me.

JUNE: Butch, don't encourage him like that.

BUTCH: Wat? I just trying to help. Daddy need information, right? I can get 'um for him, no problem. Wen he get all da facts, he can decide wat to do.

(Sound of a car starting up.)

Aeh, Dee, wait! Aeh, aeh!

(He rushes out. GRACIE watches, then closes the door.)

JUNE: You see the trouble now? Why even think about Vegas? I know. It was Harry. He's always been a bad influence on you.

WALLY: No, no, not Harry, no blame him.

JUNE: Yes, Harry. He always used to get you in trouble.

WALLY: Wat kine trouble? Wen?

JUNE: Years ago, I remember when you and Harry went to the cock-fights and the police raided the place.

WALLY: Oh dat. Dat wasn't Harry's fault. Blame Aki Kamiya for dat. He da one wen' take Harry and me to da cockfights. Gracie, you neva hear dis before but dat time I was so scared I almost kukae in my pants.

JUNE: Mama was really worried when you didn't come home.

WALLY (to GRACIE and ALVIN): Well, see, da t'ree of us wen' out in one truck wit' some odda guys, way out Wahiawa side deep in da cane-fields. So we was watching da chickens fight wen we hear cars come up and was da police. Ho, we haul ass oudda dere, man. Everybody wen' scatta all ova da place. I was running t'rough da sugar cane wit'

Harry and Aki. Oh, heart attack, heart attack all da way. Finally we
came out and found one road. Took us hellava long time come back
to Honolulu. But we was lucky. One buta kaukau man wen' come—

GRACIE: One wat?

WALLY: One buta kaukau man, one a dose guys who go around picking
up pig slop from people. He wen' give us a ride in da back a da truck
wit' all da pig slop.

JUNE: You should've seen him. The buttons on his shirt were gone, dirt
all over his face and clothes. And he was so smelly.

WALLY: Wat you expect? Pig slop not perfume, you know. But dat time,
Harry wen' actually save me. Wit'out his help, da police catch me
sure.

JUNE: And if you go to Vegas, the police there will arrest you someday
with Harry and his wild ideas. Daddy, you're happy in Hawai'i. Be
sensible. You think you could have fun in Vegas. For a short time,
yes, but then you'll get bored. You can't gamble all the time. And if
you do, you'll lose everything like the Murata man. I don't care what
you say about control. Gambling can become a disease.

WALLY: Hmmm, I get one headache. I going in my bedroom rest.
*(WALLY exits. There is a long pause. ALVIN looks around, then his
stomach rumbles loudly. GRACIE returns to the kitchen.)*

ALVIN: Aaaahhh, you get one nice family.

JUNE: Thank you.

ALVIN: Yeah, good you folks talk to each odda. Me, I'm da only child.
And my folks, dey not big talkas. Usually for dinna we just sit in
front of da TV and eat. My folks, dey like da Japanee programs.

JUNE: That's nice.
*(ALVIN's stomach rumbles even louder. He clears his throat and bends
over, squeezing his stomach. Just as GRACIE returns, there is another
deep rumble.)*

GRACIE: Wow, wat was dat? Sound like tunda.

JUNE: Oh, we didn't serve dinner. Vinny must be hungry.

ALVIN: No, I not hungry. For real. No worry about me.

GRACIE: In dis house, dey like one big bowl a rice and den dey pour da
stew ova. I make one for you.

JUNE: Daddy, how you feeling?

WALLY (*offstage*): Aaaaahhhh, go eat. No wait for me.

JUNE: Well, I might as well come back tomorrow and we can talk. I'm not hungry anyway. Gracie, I'm going. Nice to have met you, Vinny.

ALVIN: Ah, if you wanna talk, I like to listen. I mean, I get pretty good ears. I listen to my parents talk all da time. In fact, I listen betta dan I talk. Maybe we can go someplace and I can just listen. I don't like Vegas too.

JUNE: You don't?

ALVIN: No. I only go once a year to take my folks. I don't have any fun dere. If we go someplace to talk, I can tell you all da reasons why I hate Vegas.

JUNE: Well, we could go to . . . I guess Liliha Bakery.

ALVIN: We can go in my car.

JUNE: No, we'll go in our own cars so you don't have to drive back.

ALVIN: Okay.

GRACIE: You not going eat da stew rice?

ALVIN: We gotta go.

JUNE: Sorry, Gracie.

GRACIE: Dis da first time I stay at one dinna, and everybody go home wit'out eating.

(*WALLY peers out from upstage, then walks out. The front of his trousers is all wet.*)

WALLY: Someting is wrong wit' da faucet.

GRACIE: You like eat?

WALLY: No.

GRACIE: 'S wat I figga.

WALLY: You tink I was crazy bring up Vegas again?

GRACIE: I tought you already made up your mind dat Vegas was no good for you.

WALLY: 'S da funny part. You know wen Kay was getting weaka from da cancer, I actually tought maybe Kay and me should go live in Vegas.

GRACIE: No kidding.

WALLY: I could see Kay getting stronga and stronga in Vegas because playing da slot machines gave her da energy she neva get at home. And I tought maybe I might see one miracle.

GRACIE: So wat happen?

WALLY: Nuttin'. I neva even ask Kay if she like go live dere. Was kinna crazy idea, I guess. But wat if I wen' ask her, and she said yes? I shoulda said someting to her.

GRACIE: So wat you going do now?

WALLY: I dunno. All I know is I like do da right ting. But wat is da right ting?

(WALLY ponders as lights fade to black.)

Act Two

Scene 1

(Early evening. WALLY enters from upstage hallway in aloha shirt and trousers. Barefoot as usual. He enters the kitchen as the doorbell rings. He comes out with a small glass of orange juice and opens the door. HARRY enters and takes the glass away.)

HARRY: Aeh, too early?

WALLY: No, I like talk, das why.

HARRY: Sorry I was out wen you called last night.

WALLY: Wat you said about Vegas. Maybe I should move dere.

HARRY: Aeh, 's tarrific. 'S wat I was hoping. Wally and Harry togedda again—in Vegas. We can beat dat town.

WALLY: But June hate da idea.

HARRY: So wat? 'S your life. You cannot let your daughta tell you wat to do. She not your muddah.

WALLY: But she get level head.

HARRY: You live in Vegas, come home visit once a year. June stay in Honolulu, visit you once a year. Perfect.

WALLY: But she already forty-one. She not married. I no like leave her here alone.

HARRY: Butch like go?

WALLY: I tink he like da idea.

HARRY: Sure. Butch love Vegas.

WALLY: But den his wife DeeDee got mad.

HARRY: Chee, 's why hard wit' wahines. Dey no listen like da old days. Dey too independent today. Before, we tell 'um we going do dis, we going do dat, dey say, "Okay, honey." Now, hah! 'S why Ellen and me wen' divorce.

WALLY: So I get one big problem.

HARRY: No, you okay. June get da problem.

WALLY: If she was married, I no worry. If I know somebody taking care a her . . .

HARRY: June is not your liddle girl anymore. You going let her run your life? Do wat best for you. Wassamatta wit' da Fukuda men around here? Butch no can handle his wife?

WALLY: Well, DeeDee t'irteen years younga dan Butch, but she da boss, I tink. He depend on her plenny.

HARRY: If I talk to DeeDee, I bet I can convince her dat Vegas is a good place to live.

WALLY: 'S why I wen' invite everybody ova tonight. Besides, get plenny leftova stew.

HARRY: Good, leave it to me. Maybe I can make June see da light too.

WALLY: I dunno. She get hard head. I wonda where she get dat from? Kay was not li'dat. Kay neva complain about anyting.

HARRY: June get her hard head from you.

WALLY: Me?

HARRY: Yeah, you. Hard head bugga. Rememba way back wen I told you, forget da bakery, quit da union. Wat good? I said go start your own bakery. But you said, no, I get good job, security, da union protect me. So you work for da bakery all your life and you retire, and da bakery no give a damn about you.

WALLY: Da bakery treated me okay.

HARRY: But you coulda been your own boss. You coulda been betta dan Leonard's Bakery. You coulda been bigga dan King's Bakery. But you was hard head.

WALLY: Aeh, wit' da job, I bought dis house, I raise two kids. I was satisfied.

HARRY: No get me wrong. I happy for you. But, Wally, wat might have been, wat might have been.

WALLY: Well, too late now.

HARRY: Not too late, Wally, not too late. You only sixty-five. You get twenty mo' good years ahead. You and me can go into business togedda—in Vegas.

WALLY: Wat kine business?

HARRY: One shave-ice store.

WALLY: You nuts.

HARRY: No, listen. Vegas get real hot, you know dat. All da haoles up dere, all dey know is sno-cone. No ono dat ting. Ice too big, too chunky. Blah! We make finely shaved ice lightly packed and pour on da syrup, Hawai'i style. Or add some azuki beans or ice cream in da bottom of the cup. Da haoles going eat 'um up. And we catch all da Hawai'i gamblers from da California Hotel too.

WALLY: Nah. Where da store going be?

HARRY: Gotta be someplace where get lodda foot traffic. Maybe on Fremont Avenue near da Four Queens, Golden Nugget, Horseshoe. And da California not dat far away.

WALLY: How can make money wit' shave ice?

HARRY: Aeh, you know da Sekiya store in Aiea? 'S one popular place. No tell me dey not raking in da bucks. Tink of it. All you giving is ice and syrup and charging one dolla. Or dolla fifty if you add azuki beans or ice cream. Lodda profit dere, I tell you.

WALLY: So I go from frying doughnuts to shaving ice?

HARRY: Aeh, 's wat you get quit school in da tenth grade. 'S da payment you get for being one juvenile delinquent.

WALLY: You was worse dan me. You was expelled from Central Intermediate.

HARRY: Oh no, oh no, you not going smear my name. No sir. I was not expelled. I was not a bad boy. I was a stupid boy. I wen' flunk out. Nyyyyaaahhh!

(GRACIE and ALVIN enter at front door.)

HARRY: Hi, Gracie.

GRACIE: You guys talking about Vegas?

HARRY: No, I was asking Wally if I get chance wit' you.

GRACIE: Sure. We can fool around, and wen my Teddy come back from Guam, he going chop you up in one million pieces.

HARRY: Oh, I know you like my body but no come too close.

WALLY: Harry, I like you meet Vinny, June's boyfriend.

ALVIN: I'm not really her—

HARRY: Vinny. Vinny Testaverde!

ALVIN: No, Kawabata.

HARRY: You get Italian blood?

ALVIN: No, just plain Japanese.

HARRY: You know, I got a buddy in Vegas, big shot executive at Caesars, Vinny Serritelli. Sharp guy. Wally, any time you wanna see a show at Caesars, leave it to me.

WALLY: Vinny and June wen' out on one date already.

ALVIN: Well, not one real date.

WALLY: Everyting wen' okay?

ALVIN: Oh, we had a nice talk.

WALLY: Now forget I'm her faddah. But you like June?

ALVIN: Oh, she's a real good girl. I neva meet one good girl like her before. So I asked her if I could take her out.

WALLY: And she said . . . ?

ALVIN: Okay.

WALLY: Vinny own one fish market.

ALVIN: Oh, dis ogo and dis menpachi.

(He hands over two packages. GRACIE takes the packages from WALLY and goes into the kitchen.)

WALLY: Chee, t'anks. Menpachi hard to get.

ALVIN: I get one secret source. No ask me who. Cannot leak out.

HARRY: I promise if you tell me da secret, I no tell nobody.

ALVIN: Okay, but you gotta —

WALLY: No, no, you no need tell Harry.

HARRY: Aeh, Alvin, no mo' one decent fish market in Vegas. If you can swing 'um, you can make plenny money in Vegas. I can get people like Wayne Newton come ova give you business.

ALVIN: You know Wayne Newton?

HARRY: My buddy. Weneva he do one show, I always go backstage see him. He tell me, "Aeh, Harry, nice to see ya, you're my good luck charm." Watta guy. He gives da best show in town.

GRACIE: Wally, you like eat dinna outside? Nice tonight.

WALLY: Yeah, good idea.

GRACIE: Okay, I take da tings outside.

HARRY: Aeh, you wen' fix da backyard, eh?

WALLY: I put up one barbecue.

HARRY: Nice.

(GRACIE exits with dishes. HARRY follows her outside.)

ALVIN: June was saying you used to go see da Asahi and Red Sox teams play at Honolulu Stadium.

WALLY: I used to go every weekend back in da forties and fifties.

ALVIN: Me too. We lived McCully side and my muddah made musubi for me, and I put Delaware Punch in dis old Army canteen and I sat in da right-field bleachers.

WALLY: Is dat right? You know, dose teams was not pros but dey played good baseball. Just regular working guys but I bet some a dem coulda played Triple A ball.

(*HARRY returns.*)

Aeh, Vinny used to see da Red Sox and Asahis play.

HARRY: Honolulu Stadium, first-base grandstand seats, my fav'rite place. Cannot beat dose days, yeah.

WALLY: Wat was your fav'rite team?

ALVIN: Da Asahis. Victor Mori, Dick Kashiwaeda, Tets Omiya, Larry Kameshima . . .

WALLY: Wait, wait, no can beat da Red Sox wit' Majo Uyehara.

HARRY: 'S was our team. Dose days we neva get major league baseball on TV, so da local playas were our heroes.

WALLY: First base Masa Gunda.

HARRY: Second base Tsune Watanabe.

WALLY: Shortstop Larry Yaji.

HARRY: Hooo, dat guy was smood. Slicka, man, slicka.

WALLY: T'ird base Shin Yogi.

ALVIN: Yeah, Shin Yogi. I tought he was related to Yogi Berra.

WALLY: Aeh, da ball hit deep to short, Yaji (*playing it out*) scoop 'um up, sidearm to Watanabe at second . . .

(*HARRY makes the catch and hurls to ALVIN, who is surprised but catches the phantom ball clumsily.*)

HARRY: And on to first to Gunda.

WALLY: Good catch, Gunda.

HARRY: Double play. Aeh, dose guys were betta dan Tinkers to Evers to Chance. Yaji to Watanabe to Gunda.

WALLY: Aeh, aeh, outfield.

HARRY: Left field Kats Kojima.

WALLY: Centa field Toku Tanaka.

HARRY: Right field Riki Watanabe, Tsune's bruddah.

WALLY: No forget da pitcha and catcha.

HARRY: Of course not. Catching, da great Sol Kaulukukui.

WALLY: And pitching, da fantastic Jimmy Doole.

HARRY: Kaulukukui and Doole, two great guys.

WALLY: Dose two was da only non-Japanese on da Red Sox, I tink, but dey was da heart and soul of da team.

HARRY: Last but not least, da manager Peanuts Kunihisa.

WALLY: Dat man was sharp, no nonsense kinna guy. He coulda managed in da major leagues.

HARRY: But, you know, I tink da best Hawai'i playa I eva saw was Wally Yonamine. Da guy was oudda dis world. All-star in baseball and football . . .

WALLY: Made da Japan baseball Hall of Fame. Wow, 's someting.

HARRY: 'S was da good fun time. Now no mo' Honolulu Stadium. I love dat old place. Hawai'i really junk nowdays. 'S why I love Vegas. Hawai'i change too much. Mo' crime, mo' murders, mo' traffic, mo' homeless. Aeh, I went to A'ala Park look around. Was so sad wen I see some homeless people sleeping in da park, lying around like dey sick or someting. Pitiful. (to ALVIN) Wen I was young, A'ala Park was one lively place. Used to get softball games on weekends wit' special men teams, even wahine teams, and dey had deir own uniforms too. Lodda people would come watch dem play. Big crowds. Real festive atmosphere. Today A'ala Park look so small, so diff'rent. Get da sign A'ala Street, but no mo' street. All covered up wit' grass. A'ala Street used to have tenements and lodda stores making business. Today nuttin'. I wonda where all da people went. Now A'ala Park so sad, so quiet. No mo' life. You see, Wally, 's why you betta come to Vegas. Not our Hawai'i anymore.

WALLY: I guess da old days always look betta dan da present. Nostalgia, yeah.

HARRY: Nostalgia nuttin'. Reality. Da old days were betta. But no can go back. So we gotta find one nodda place to live.

WALLY: But Hawai'i still get da aloha spirit.

HARRY: So, we get lodda Hawai'i people living in Vegas, we get our own aloha spirit dere.

(DEEDEE enters at the front door.)

DEEDEE: Hi, everybody.

WALLY: Hi, DeeDee. Where Butch?

DEEDEE: I came in my own car. I wanted to talk to you first.

WALLY: Someting wrong?

DEEDEE: No, but, ah . . .

HARRY: Aeh, Vinny, we go outside wit' Gracie, give her bad time.

(*They go out.*)

WALLY: Wassamatta?

DEEDEE: Butch serious about moving to Vegas wit' you.

WALLY: 'S good, eh? Wat about you?

DEEDEE: I worry about Butch up dere.

WALLY: He can find one job easy.

DEEDEE: Not dat. His gambling.

WALLY: He's a smart gambler. I made sure about dat.

DEEDEE: But he no mo' control sometimes. Last year at his high school reunion in Vegas, he lost almost t'ree tousand.

WALLY: Dat much? He neva told me.

DEEDEE: I know. I guess he was embarrassed. Rememba around dat time he had to borrow one tousand from you.

WALLY: He said his car transmission wen' broke.

DEEDEE: And I asked my faddah for one tousand to help pay da apartment rent. Wat gonna happen if Butch live in Vegas all time? Too tempting for him. He can be just like one kid sometimes.

WALLY: But he lose dat big only dat one time, right?

DEEDEE: Dat's da most he lost at one time, but he hardly come home a winna.

WALLY: I always tought he did pretty good.

DEEDEE: He tell you wen he win, but wen he lose, he neva tell you da real amount.

WALLY: Yeah, yeah, lodda gamblers do dat. I shoulda figga dat out. DeeDee, I like you and Butch come live wit' me in Vegas. Going be one big house so you folks can have lodda space. And Butch's gambling, I make sure he no go crazy. I keep my eye on him. And if you see anyting, you let me know right away.

(*BUTCH rushes in.*)

BUTCH: Aeh, Daddy, wateva she said, no believe her. She dunno wat she talking about.

WALLY: She said you da handsomest guy she eva saw.

BUTCH: Well, I neva said she was blind.

(*DEEDEE exits to backyard.*)

BUTCH: DeeDee and me was talking last night. I ready to go wit' you to Vegas. But she kinna scared. She neva live no place but Hawai'i.

WALLY: Butch, if we go up, you can handle da gambling?

BUTCH: No problem. I mean, wat, sometimes you win, sometimes you lose. But you gotta have control, right? 'S wat you always say.

WALLY: I know, but you get control?

BUTCH: Yeah, just like you, Daddy. Control, man, control.

WALLY: I no like cause you trouble.

BUTCH: No trouble, Daddy. No trouble. We going be togedda in Vegas. Start one new life. Maybe Dee can get pregnant dere. We been trying long time to get one baby. Maybe Hawai'i no good for her body rhythms or someting. Maybe desert air betta for her.

WALLY: If I go, I like buy one t'ree- or four-bedroom house, and I like you and DeeDee come live wit' me.

BUTCH: 'S good, sure, gotta stick togedda.

WALLY: I like June come too, but . . .

BUTCH: You know June, eh, she get education so she tink she know all da answers. Let her stay in Honolulu. She probably going be one old maid but . . . *(shrugs)*

(HARRY returns.)

HARRY: Aeh, Butch.

(He hands a can of beer to BUTCH. They do the local handshake smoothly.)

BUTCH: Wat you say, Harry.

HARRY: Going be good, going be good.

BUTCH: Ready, man, ready.

HARRY: I was telling DeeDee I can help her find one job. Secretary, eh? Easy, brah, easy. One a da hotels can hire her. Leave it to me.

BUTCH: T'anks. Dat going be one big help.

HARRY: Aeh, brah, aeh, 's wat friends are for. Excuse, eh, I gotta use da bat'room.

WALLY: Oh wait. Butch, I like you check da bat'room faucet. Funny kine.

BUTCH: Wassamatta?

WALLY: Try come look.

HARRY: Aeh, aeh, let me use da toilet first, eh.

(All three head off upstage. JUNE enters at front door. She doesn't look happy. ALVIN enters from backyard.)

ALVIN: June.

JUNE: Hello, Vinny.

ALVIN: I brought da ogo and menpachi I promised you. I gave 'um to your faddah.

JUNE: Oh you didn't have to. Expensive those things.

ALVIN: No, I was happy to bring 'um—for you.

JUNE: It was nice of you to listen to me the last time. Must've been boring for you.

ALVIN: Oh no. Betta dan watching Japanee programs wit' my muddah and faddah. By da time I close up da market, go home, wash up, eat dinna, it's pretty late. I don't have time to go out much, so being wit' you was good, different.

JUNE: Well, I won't bend your ear tonight.

ALVIN: You can bend my ears all you like. I get tough ears.

(HARRY *returns.*)

HARRY: Hello, June.

JUNE: Harry.

HARRY: Good to see you. Your father and I are having a great time recalling our youth. Even Vinny here remembers those times. Right, Vinny?

ALVIN: Oh yeah. I was young, but I didn't forget.

(WALLY *is back.*)

WALLY: Gracie, where you put da monkey wrench?

GRACIE (*offstage*): Unda da kitchen sink.

(WALLY *heads for the kitchen.*)

WALLY: Oh, June, good, good.

(*He exits.*)

HARRY: How are things?

JUNE: Good. And you?

HARRY: Couldn't be better. Las Vegas is always jumping. Can't believe that city. About six thousand people move to Vegas every month. Fastest-growing city in the country.

JUNE: Do you work for the Chamber of Commerce there?

HARRY: No. But that's not a bad idea. They should pay me for all the good things I say about the city. Then I come back to Honolulu and see A'ala Park and all those homeless people, I think, what's going on? Where did all those homeless come from, where are they going?

JUNE: You could take them to Vegas with you.

HARRY: No, we don't want losers in Vegas, only winners.

JUNE: I bet there are more losers than winners there.

HARRY: It's a bet. And I win. 'Cause, you see, to be a winner, in Vegas, you don't have to come home with jackpot money. All you gotta do is have a good time with friends or family. It's sharing a common purpose: to hit the jackpot. Sometimes you win, sometimes you don't. But it's still fun and you can forget your troubles at least for the time being. Vegas is the place where adult children take their elderly parents to play because it's the Magic Kingdom. Old folks in wheelchairs with daughters pushing them along. It's a son bringing his elderly parents to the slot machines for the first time and showing them how to play. And feeling great when his parents really enjoy themselves. And when they hit the jackpot, the son feels like crying because he made his parents laugh and be happy, something he was never able to do at home. That son was me. I wish my parents were still alive 'cause I would take them to Vegas with me to live and I would take them to the California Hotel every day just so I could see them having fun.

ALVIN: Maybe I should take my parents to Vegas more often.

WALLY (emerging): Oh, Vinny, try come. I like you show Butch wat wen' happen wen you wet your pants dat night.

(ALVIN exits with WALLY.)

HARRY: How's your father taking retirement?

JUNE: He was doing great until you put the idea in his head about moving to Vegas.

HARRY: I think it would be good for him. Few years ago when I hit fifty-five, I sold my home and moved to Vegas, and I never regretted what I did. Even after I split everything with my ex-wife, it was still worth it. Your father could make a bigger financial gain than me.

JUNE: It's not the money. He's comfortable enough. He has family and friends here.

HARRY: I'll be there. I'll help him.

JUNE: That's the trouble. You're a bad influence, Harry. I don't want you to corrupt him.

HARRY: No, June, you got it wrong. I would never do anything to hurt Wally. I guess he never told you, but he sorta saved my life long time ago. I was a kid who had flunked out of school and I was bumming around A'ala Park wasting my life. Your father noticed me in the park and became like a big brother. He even gave me money so I could eat and encouraged me, all this after my own father kicked me out of the house. If it wasn't for your father, I don't know what would've happened to me. I got a lot to thank Wally for, and I'll always look out for him.

(*WALLY and ALVIN return, followed later by BUTCH.*)

WALLY: Now you can use da bat'room and no need worry about wetting your pants again. C'mon, everybody, we go eat. Harry, les go.

(*WALLY, ALVIN, and HARRY exit to backyard.*)

JUNE: Butch.

BUTCH: Wat?

JUNE: I like talk.

BUTCH: You not hungry? We go eat first.

JUNE: No, wait. Harry's trying hard to get Daddy to move to Vegas.

BUTCH: I know.

JUNE: Well, what do you think?

BUTCH: Aeh, I like da idea. I hope Dee and me can go too. Daddy tinking of getting one big house so we can live wit' him.

JUNE: Don't you care, leaving all your friends in Hawai'i?

BUTCH: You crazy? I going see my friends mo' often 'cause dey always visiting Vegas. Daddy's house going be one busy place wit' his friends stopping by and my friends coming. Hell, we going be having parties all da time. If you smart, you come too. Make Daddy happy. In fact, if you go too, no question Daddy going.

JUNE: I don't want to go.

BUTCH: Aeh, 's okay wit' me. But you can find some kinna teaching job in Vegas, and you no mo' husband or boyfriend here so you no mo' reason to stay.

(*BUTCH goes out to backyard. JUNE sits dejectedly as GRACIE comes in.*)

GRACIE: June, come eat.

JUNE: Now Butch wants to go to Vegas.

GRACIE: 'S no eart'shaka. I would be surprised if you wanted to go.

JUNE: Doesn't Daddy see it's a stupid idea?

GRACIE: Well, if he go, not going be da same wit'out him.

JUNE: You're on my side, aren't you? You don't want my father to go.

GRACIE: Betta for me if he stay in Hawai'i. I would miss him. But, you know, he not da only one. Lodda people leaving Hawai'i. Dey feel like Hawai'i got nuttin' to offer anymore. Especially good jobs. It's pretty sad.

JUNE: But it's different with Daddy. He just retired and he has no worries about things like job or taking care of the family. I don't know what he's thinking. Is he worried about anything?

GRACIE: Well, he is worried about you.

JUNE: Me? He's so silly.

GRACIE: I know. He get in his fuzzy little head dat you need one husband.

JUNE: He's so old-fashioned. He can't understand that a woman doesn't have to be married to be happy. What does Daddy want me to do— marry some fool with no manners just so he can move to Vegas?

GRACIE: Yeah, it's funny about faddahs and daughtas. My faddah was like Wally. He cared about me more dan his own life. Maybe dat's why I feel so close to Wally. It's such a good feeling, yeah, wen your faddah love you dat much.

JUNE: Well, if he loves me that much, he won't go to Vegas.

GRACIE: But, you know, June, in a way Wally is right. Faddah and daughta is diff'rent than husband and wife. I loved my faddah wit' all my heart, but wen Teddy came into my life, everyting wen' change. I was no longa daddy's liddle girl looking up to him. Wit' me and Teddy, it was like equal partnas on da same level. I was a woman. And a damn good one too. And wen you get your husband in da sack, and you make love, and it's good, well, 's someting you cannot get from a faddah. It's like real fulfillment. Fulfillment? Aeh, how did I come up wit' dat word. Surprise me.

JUNE: I know, Gracie, but you were lucky to find Teddy. There are no Teddys in my life.

GRACIE: Aeh, no get me wrong. Teddy is no carnival prize. In fact, he was da runt of da litter. But he was my runt.

JUNE: Maybe I am selfish. But I don't want Daddy to leave. I have to take care of him. He needs me. He has to see that. It's wrong to move to Vegas. He can't go. I won't let him.

(Lights fade to black.)

Scene 2

(Later that night. DEEDEE *and* BUTCH *enter from back door.)*

BUTCH: Everyting going change wen we go to Vegas.

DEEDEE: How?

BUTCH: Well, for one ting, we going make our baby dere.

(He tries to grab her.)

DEEDEE: Aeh, no touch.

BUTCH *(singsong)*: We going make one baby, we going make one baby.

DEEDEE: And if da baby don't come, den wat?

BUTCH: Gotta come 'cause important to me. One boy to keep up da Fukuda name. I going do good in Vegas. Maybe start out as one security guard, yeah, but I can do mo' dan dat. Living in Hawai'i was holding me back. You just wait. Aeh, and Harry going be one big help. He get connections. 'S wat we need. You know da right people, you move up.

DEEDEE: But wat if dere's no baby?

BUTCH: Aeh, wat you talking about? Da docta said you can have ten babies. We going make us one baby and we going have fun while we make da baby. *(He embraces and kisses her.)* We go in my old bedroom.

DEEDEE: No. Everybody going be looking for us.

BUTCH: Who cares?

DEEDEE: Not tonight.

BUTCH: Why?

DEEDEE: 'Cause you putting pressure on me. I don't wanna make love unda pressure.

BUTCH: Pressure about wat?

DEEDEE: Da baby.

BUTCH: Okay, tonight no count. Going count only wen we get to Vegas. Tonight only for fun.

DEEDEE: You love me?

BUTCH: Aaaahhh . . . yeah.

DEEDEE: Why do you love me?

BUTCH: Dis one trick question?

DEEDEE: No. Just tell me why and be honest.

BUTCH: Okay, okay. I love you because you da only one I can make laugh. Nobody else like my liddle jokes. I love you because you always tink mo' about me dan about yourself. And I can brag to you about wat I did and you always listen and you always so happy for me. I love you because . . . I love you.

(DEEDEE kisses BUTCH. JUNE enters.)

JUNE: Butch, I want to talk with you.

BUTCH: Well, Dee and I gotta do someting.

JUNE: It's important. It's about Daddy.

BUTCH: I know wat you going say. But if Daddy wanna move to Vegas, 's his business. He's not a kid.

JUNE: Don't you see? It's not about moving to Vegas, it's about leaving Hawai'i—our home, our life, our culture.

BUTCH: Aeh, Hawai'i going downhill. No mo' opportunities here. Tourism hitting hard times. Cost of living is high. Not just retirees heading for Vegas. Lodda younga people going too. So if Daddy wanna live in Vegas, well, Dee and I willing to go wit' him.

JUNE: But what if Daddy gets sick or something, we gotta stick together.

BUTCH: If someting happen to Daddy, I can take care a him. I going be wit' him, so no worry. Trust me. See, I no blame you, you like stay in Honolulu. Schoolteacha, steady job. And you like Daddy stay in Hawai'i wit' you, but maybe Hawai'i not da best place for Daddy. Dee, I going lie down wait for you. No take too long.

(BUTCH exits to bedroom.)

JUNE: Well, I guess you can hardly wait to go to Sin City too.

DEEDEE: Not really. But Butch wanna go so badly. And I don't wanna lose him. I'm willing to go. But he keeps bugging me about having a baby.

JUNE: Yeah, I hear him too, like a stuck record. It's an obsession with him.

DEEDEE: Da thing is, he doesn't have enough tadpoles in his juice.

JUNE: Not enough tadpoles in his juice? What?

DEEDEE: Yeah, you know, he's not a baby maker. 'S wat da doctor said. He was gonna tell Butch, but I said I would tell him. Dat would really hurt Butch. So he doesn't know.

JUNE: Even if he did know, he wouldn't believe it. I guess that's why he divorced Miriam. He thought she couldn't give him a baby. But it was his fault all along. Men are such fools.

DEEDEE: Wat I going do about Butch?

JUNE: He's so macho, he's pathetic. You're too good for him.

DEEDEE: But I love him.

JUNE: Dee, Butch is a lucky guy.

(*JUNE puts an arm around* DEEDEE. ALVIN *enters.*)

ALVIN: Boy, your faddah and Harry sure know lodda stories. Dey having a good time out dere.

JUNE: They've been friends a long time.

ALVIN: I wish I had a friend like dat.

JUNE: You don't want a friend like Harry.

ALVIN: No, I mean your faddah. He's a good guy.

JUNE: Yes, he's special.

(DEEDEE *exits to bedroom.*)

ALVIN: Ah, he probably would make a nice faddah-in-law.

JUNE: DeeDee gets along with him.

ALVIN: His oxtail stew was ono. You helped him make 'um?

JUNE: I don't cook. I never learned.

ALVIN: How come?

JUNE: I didn't want to.

ALVIN: Oh. How you eat?

JUNE: I buy things. Take-out. Frozen dinners. They're fine.

ALVIN: I guess so.

JUNE: Most men I dated didn't like it that I couldn't cook. All they wanted was a maid to clean the house and cook their meals.

ALVIN: I cook pretty good.

JUNE: Doesn't your mother cook at home?

ALVIN: Oh yeah. But she's getting old, so I cook lodda times, mostly on weekends. I like cooking. I don't mind if my wife can't cook.

JUNE: Well, that shows you're not tied down to old-fashioned notions. You're not afraid of exhibiting your "female" traits.

ALVIN: You mean—I'm a sissy?

JUNE: No, you're a man, a real man. Deep inside, I mean. You're not one of those superficial he-man phonies.

(DEEDEE *returns.*)

DEEDEE: Butch sleeping like a baby.

(*She continues out to the backyard.*)

JUNE: The only thing wrong with you is your name.

ALVIN: Yeah, I know. Kawabata, wat a name.

JUNE: Kawabata is fine. It's Vinny. Doesn't suit you.

ALVIN: Well, it's not my real name.

JUNE: Why do they call you Vinny?

ALVIN: Your faddah gave me dat name. He didn't like my real name—
Alvin.

JUNE: I like Alvin better.

ALVIN: You do? Well, I can change 'um back real easy.

(*The others return from the backyard.*)

DEEDEE: Getting late. I betta go.

WALLY: Where Butch?

DEEDEE: Sleeping. No wake him up. Bye-bye, everybody.

WALLY: DeeDee, no worry. Everyting going be okay. I promise.

(*She exits.*)

GRACIE: Vinny, you like go too or you getting too much fun?

JUNE: His name isn't Vinny, so please everyone stop calling him that.
His name is Alvin.

HARRY: Alvin? Alvin is one squirrel, right?

GRACIE: No, chipmunk.

JUNE: See now, don't tease him. You mustn't tease. It's not good manners. I think you should all apologize to Alvin.

HARRY (*aside to WALLY*): I forgot June is a teacher.

WALLY: Sorry, Alvin. My fault, yeah.

HARRY: No harm, eh, Alvin.

GRACIE: Alvin, I going now, you too?

ALVIN: I guess so.

HARRY: Me too. Wally, I can use your phone? Gotta call one taxi.

ALVIN: No need. I take you.

HARRY: You sure? I staying at da Halekulani.

ALVIN: Yeah, we go.

HARRY: Okay, t'anks . . . Alvin.

(*WALLY and JUNE go to the door to say goodbye.*)

ALVIN: Can I call you next week?

JUNE: Yes.

HARRY: Bye-bye, everybody. Good to see all of you. Next time Vegas.

GRACIE: Good night, sleep tight.

ALVIN: T'anks for everyting, Wally.

WALLY: Okay, Alvin, no mention.

(They leave.)

If Butch no wake up, I guess I let him sleep ova. You like stay too? Your bedroom is clean.

JUNE: Hmmmm. I wish it was thirty years ago, and Mama was still young and healthy. I didn't think so at the time, but those were the best years. Carefree and simple. You and Mama were always there to watch over Butch and me. We had fun then too, didn't we? *(WALLY nods.)* I still remember the time you brought home lots and lots of crabs, and Mama boiled them all in two huge pots. We had so much crab meat, Mama froze a lot for crab salads and other stuff. But that night we spread newspapers on the living room floor and got out two nutcrackers and two hammers. And we sat around cracking open the crabs and eating with our fingers. Was ono. Remember?

WALLY: Of course. No can forget da kine stuff. Dat was one special night.

JUNE: Mama was in such a happy mood. She laughed so hard when you hit your finger with the hammer.

WALLY: Aeh, dat really hurt.

JUNE: Oh Daddy, sometimes I wish I were a kid again and I could sit on your lap and tell you all about the things I did in school.

WALLY: Yeah, you too big now. I wish Mama was here too.

JUNE: Yes. Then I could learn to cook from Mama. She wanted to teach me, but I was so stubborn. I never cared to cook.

WALLY: Not too late to learn.

JUNE: It wouldn't be the same without Mama. If she were here now, I would say, "Mama, show me how to make your ono sushi."

WALLY: You was one tomboy, wat you going do.

JUNE: I guess it's not just making sushi or anything else, but it's like mother and daughter sharing things.

(WALLY picks up a jigsaw piece, which he fits into the puzzle.)

WALLY: Liddle bit mo' and I can finish dis puzzle. Mama no help me, 's why I get hard time.

JUNE: Tell me about wen you and Mama were newlyweds.

WALLY: Newlyweds? I dunno. Wat I can say? Nuttin' special.

JUNE: Try.

WALLY: Well . . . aaahhhh, I dunno.

JUNE: Daddy, before you two got married then.

WALLY: Well, I came back from Europe afta da army. And I was really broke ass. So I used to hang out Aʻala Park side. Dere was dis small saimin stand. Was one shack. Da walls was all old termite. Da roof was corrugated metal. But from da outside, I could smell da barbecue meat cooking on da charcoal grill. I can still smell ʼum. So I wenʼ in eat saimin. Hooo, da ono. Da best saimin I eva had. Maybe because your muddah wenʼ serve me. She was da waitress. So young and nice and pretty. I was going pay but I found one big puka in my pants pocket. I dunno wen I wenʼ lose my money. I neva can pay. I was so shame. So I told your muddah wat happen, and I tought she going be so mad, but she only laugh, laugh, laugh. She had da best laugh in da world. And so nice. Made me feel good. She paid da bill witʼ her own money. I knew den she was da girl I going marry.

JUNE: Mama never told me.

WALLY: Kinna personal, eh. Was our own story between her and me. But now she no stay, so I guess okay to tell.

JUNE: Oh Daddy, I wish Iʼd been at that saimin stand with you and Mama.

WALLY: Kinna hard, eh. You was still in heaven waiting to be born.

JUNE: Life was so much simpler those days.

WALLY: Yep. Lodda memories. ʼS da ting, yeah. I can take dose memories witʼ me to Vegas.

JUNE: Daddy, you cannot think about moving to Vegas. Not after what you just said.

WALLY: Wat I said?

JUNE: Your whole life, Mamaʼs life, the two of you in Hawaiʻi. You canʼt.

WALLY: But I told Harry I going.

JUNE: Tell him you changed your mind.

WALLY: I dunno.

JUNE: What about me? Donʼt you want to stay here with me? Donʼt I count in your life?

WALLY: Not dat. You dunno, ʼs why.

JUNE: Know what? Tell me.

WALLY: You da one I worry about da most. I no like leave you behind all alone.

JUNE: Then don't go.

WALLY: How about you come wit' Butch and me?

JUNE: No. That's ridiculous. What about Mama? How would she feel?

WALLY: If Mama was still alive, I no go Vegas.

JUNE: Daddy, what about Mama's grave?

WALLY: I come back once a year visit. And you going stay.

JUNE: I'm staying 'cause Hawai'i is our home. We belong here, not on da Mainland. The Fukuda family has been in Hawai'i a hundred years.

WALLY: Wen I die, Butch can bring my ashes back, so we going be here foreva and eva.

JUNE: It's not that.

WALLY: 'S all I care about. I going be buried in da family plot wit' Mama in Oahu Cemetery. Nice place, in da shade unda da big tree.

JUNE: If you go to the Mainland, you're going to forget Mama.

(WALLY *pauses and ponders.*)

WALLY: No, Mama is always wit' me. Every place I look. Mama doing da dishes. Mama knitting and watching TV. Mama in da backyard watering da plants. Mama trying to do da puzzle. Mama sick in bed, dying in bed. Every time I see her li'dat, I feel so sorry for her, I feel like crying. Why she hadda suffa, wen was all my fault?

JUNE: What you mean?

WALLY: Because of me, she wen' die. I wen' kill her.

JUNE: Don't be silly.

WALLY: 'S wat she said.

JUNE: Mama wouldn't have said that.

WALLY: She did. Wen she was real sick, toward da end, she said, "You wen' kill me."

JUNE: She must've been delirious. She didn't mean what she said.

WALLY: I know dat. She was not one mean person. She neva wanted to hurt me. But, you dunno how hard. I cannot sleep in da bedroom. I sleep on da couch every night. No, I cannot forget Mama. She always wit' me, day and night. If I no go Vegas, I tink I going die.

JUNE: Stop talking like that.

WALLY: But you no undastand. Mama was right. I did kill her. Wen we went to see Dr. Wada, he said da smoke from my cigarettes gave her da lung cancer. Mama used to always say, "No smoke, Daddy, bad for you." And me, stupid, I said, "Die, die, ma-ke, ma-ke." So I wen' live and Mama got sick and die in my place. I was da smoka. Was not fair to Mama. I wish I wen' die instead of her.

JUNE: No, Daddy. Mama didn't blame you. She was always worrying about you, even when she was sick, worried about what would happen to you after she was gone. She told me that. I told her I would watch over you.

WALLY: Mama loved Vegas. She even had her fav'rite slot machine. I can see her laughing wen she hit da jackpot. She had so much fun. I gotta go dere. I not going forget her. How can? She going be wit' me in Vegas all da time, cranking da slot machines, hitting da jackpots, laughing, smiling. And wen I win, I can tell Mama, "See, you gave me good luck again, Mama, you always give me good luck."

JUNE: Daddy . . .

(*There is a quiet moment, then* BUTCH *shuffles in sleepily.*)

BUTCH: Everybody wen' home?

(*He continues on to the kitchen, then returns.*)

Daddy, I going sleep in my old bed tonight. You know, da room still get da same smell. Mama smell. Her smell. Like wen I was one kid. Huh. Make me feel good.

(*He exits. Lights fade slowly to black.*)

Scene 3

(*In the darkness, we hear a scraping sound across the stage. Lights go up and there's* WALLY *pushing a large box of clothes into the living room. Another smaller box is already onstage.* WALLY, *dressed in an aloha shirt and dark trousers, looks around pensively. He takes a painting off the wall and studies it, then blows on it to remove dust.* GRACIE *enters from the backyard and watches* WALLY, *who puts the painting on the dining table.*)

GRACIE: Not finish packing yet?

WALLY: Oh. Nah, Butch going pack everyting for me.

GRACIE: You happy you flying to Vegas today?

WALLY: You know me. I neva going be happy, happy, happy.

GRACIE: I neva tink you going sell da house so quick.

WALLY: T'ree months is quick? I dunno how long supposed to take. Gotta find one nice new house in Vegas fast so Butch and DeeDee can come right away. No forget, eh, you gotta come visit me so I no get lonesome.

GRACIE: I going miss you, Wallace Fukuda.

WALLY: Aahhh, Vegas is only one short plane ride away.

GRACIE: But June is right. We cannot lose people like you to da Mainland. If everybody move to Vegas, who going be left in Hawai'i?

WALLY: Well, I gotta leave June behind.

GRACIE: She and Alvin been dating—wat you tink about dem?

WALLY: I dunno. Wit' my jigsaw puzzles, sometimes I lock da pieces togedda even t'ough no fit perfect. So I look at Alvin and I tink maybe he get chance. He no mo' pimples, right?

GRACIE: Right.

WALLY: He not bolohead.

GRACIE: Yeah, he get hair.

WALLY: And I check his teet'. Not crooked.

GRACIE: Straight like one white picket fence.

WALLY: And he not one big bamboola.

GRACIE: He's perfect.

WALLY: But June is real particular. So why she been dating him?

GRACIE: You cannot tell about wahine. I tink she sees someting in Alvin you cannot see.

WALLY: Beauty is in da eye of da beholda. Only ting June gotta get her eyes checked.

GRACIE: Wally, you bad.

WALLY: Nah, nah, nah, only kidding. Alvin is one good guy. And I give you all da credit. Afta all, you wen' bring dem togedda.

GRACIE: Aeh, no put dat ova my head, wat if no turn out good?

WALLY: Well, at least she wen' date one guy for t'ree months. 'S da longest I can rememba.

GRACIE: I report on dem for you.

WALLY: T'anks, eh. Well, wen I get to Vegas, I going hang out wit' Harry. Going be good.

GRACIE: You sure Harry not da Devil?

WALLY: Wat?

GRACIE: Sometimes da Devil can take human form, you know.

WALLY: Harry is my best friend from way back. I trust him.

GRACIE: Well, take care. Vegas is dangerous.

WALLY: Not for me. Rememba, control. Cool head main ting.

(*BUTCH and DEEDEE enter at the front door.*)

BUTCH: Hi, hi, hi. Ready?

WALLY: I been ready since five dis morning.

DEEDEE: Nervous?

WALLY: Nah. Sorry I leaving you folks all da packing.

BUTCH: Easy, easy. Neva forget nuttin'?

WALLY: Get my bags. Get my wallet. Travelers checks. Oh, I stay label all da stuff so you know wat to do.

BUTCH: Good, good. Can hardly wait till we come up. Gracie, come wit' us.

GRACIE: No, somebody gotta stay home watch da store.

DEEDEE: Harry sent me material about being a real estate agent. I tink I can do it.

WALLY: Sure you can. You know why? 'Cause you get nice personality, you get good head—

BUTCH: And people going believe you wen you sell dem worthless desert land.

WALLY: Aeh, no kid about da kine. DeeDee, you not going regret moving. You and Butch going do real good, I can feel it.

(*JUNE and ALVIN enter at the front door.*)

WALLY: Aeh, Alvin, how come? Store not open?

ALVIN: I get one helper today. I wanted to come see you. And I brought smoked ahi you can take on da plane wit' you.

WALLY: You know, I going miss all da good stuff you always give me. I no mo' nuttin' for you.

ALVIN: Well, get someting but . . .

WALLY: Tell me and I give 'um to you.

ALVIN: I take June.

WALLY: Wat?

ALVIN: Oh, ah, I dunno wat I just said, so forget everyting.

WALLY: Alvin, Alvin, not up to me anyway. You gotta ask June.

JUNE: Daddy, don't embarrass him.

WALLY: Wat I said? I neva do nuttin'.

JUNE: Sorry we didn't get here sooner. But we were with Alvin's parents earlier this morning.

WALLY: How da folks, Alvin?

ALVIN: Good. Only my muddah wen' kinna dizzy in da head wen I told her da news.

WALLY: Wat news?

ALVIN: Oh. You know, I tink I betta go to da bat'room.

JUNE: You might as well know now—I'm pregnant.

ALVIN: Wat? Who made you pregnant?

(All eyes slowly turn to ALVIN.)

BUTCH: Nah, nah.

ALVIN: I neva know wat I was doing.

(BUTCH pulls ALVIN aside.)

JUNE: Alvin and I will be getting married.

GRACIE: No wonda Mrs. Kawabata's head wen' spin.

BUTCH: If my sista was sixteen and you wen' knock her up, man, I would come rearrange your face free of charge. But since she forty-one, all I can say is: Wat da hell is your technique?

WALLY: You not doing dis because of me, for my sake?

JUNE: No. Alvin is a decent, honest, hard-working man. Any woman would be happy to marry him.

GRACIE: See, Wally, June get twenty-twenty vision.

DEEDEE *(with a hug)*: I'm so happy for you.

GRACIE *(another hug)*: Wat a wonderful surprise. It's so nice.

JUNE: I found out I was pregnant yesterday. We're going to get married in front of a judge. We don't want a fuss at our age.

ALVIN: And we going honeymoon in Arizona and Utah.

JUNE: Then we'll stop over in Vegas to see you.

WALLY: Chee, dis is like one going-away present for me. Alvin, you wen' plan dis from way back or wat?

ALVIN: No, no, I not li'dat.

JUNE: Will you show me Mama's favorite slot machine?

WALLY: My pleasure.

BUTCH: Aeh, Daddy, I no mo' good news to tell you about Dee and me. But just wait till we get to Vegas.

(He promptly elbows DEEDEE; she comes right back with a punch to his stomach.)

WALLY: Oh, June, dose boxes get Mama's clothes. You can give 'um away. I hope some people can use 'um. Okay, dat's it, I guess.

GRACIE: Wait, I like take pictures of everybody.

WALLY: Okay. Where?

GRACIE: Da couch. Wally in da middle. Two girls at his left and right. And da two guys behind.

(*They follow her instructions.*)

Dat's nice. I like da picture for remembrance. Last day togedda in dis house. I develop one for everybody. Okay, everybody, no move.

(*She snaps the picture.*)

ALVIN: Wait, lemme take one picture wit' Gracie and all of you.

WALLY: Good idea. Ah, June, come sit on my lap. Gracie, sit next to me.

(*JUNE doesn't move at first.*)

June, hurry up, bumbai I miss my plane.

(*He gives her a knowing look; she sits on his lap and hugs him. GRACIE takes her place.*)

ALVIN: Now everybody say, "Mahimahi."

EVERYBODY: Mahimahi!

ALVIN: Dat's it.

WALLY: Well, might as well go.

BUTCH: Dis two bags, 's all?

WALLY: Yep.

BUTCH: Okay, I brought my van. We can all go togedda.

JUNE: I love you, Daddy.

(*She kisses him on the cheek, then exits.*)

GRACIE: Bye-bye.

WALLY: You no like go to da airport?

GRACIE: No. Bumbai I cry like one baby.

WALLY: Okay den. Oh wait, I almost forget.

(*He rushes into the kitchen and returns with a big bakery box.*)

GRACIE: Wat dis?

WALLY: Try open.

GRACIE: Guava Chiffon Surprise!

WALLY: I made 'um special dis morning. Just for you.

(*She tries to hug him but can't because of the box. She nearly trips in putting the box on the coffee table. Returning, she embraces WALLY.*)

Well, betta go.

GRACIE: Wait, wait, you take my frog for good luck.

(*She puts the frog necklace around his neck. He looks around the house one last time.*)

WALLY: I hope da new owners take good care of dis house. Da best house I eva lived in.

(He smiles at GRACIE *and exits.* GRACIE *watches for a moment, then sits down on the couch holding the bakery box. Then she remembers something—the cassette player. She turns it on. The song "Time After Time" plays.* GRACIE *sits on the couch holding the Guava Chiffon Surprise as the song plays on. Lights slowly fade to black.)*

THE END

Aloha Las Vegas, Kumu Kahua production at Tenney Theatre, Honolulu, 1992, directed by James A. Nakamoto. Larry Fukumoto as Wally and Nan Asuncion as Gracie. PHOTO BY BRAD GODA.

Aloha Las Vegas, Kumu Kahua production at Tenney Theatre, Honolulu, 1992, directed by James A. Nakamoto. Karen Yamamoto Hackler as June and Larry Fukumoto as Wally. PHOTO BY BRAD GODA.

Aloha Las Vegas in its special limited run at the Japan America Theatre, Los Angeles, June 1994, directed by James A. Nakamoto. The original set by Joseph D. Dodd had to be somewhat modified for the production. *Left to right:* Nan Asuncion as Gracie, Meredith Rose Hill as DeeDee, Marcus Oshiro as Butch, Larry Fukumoto as Wally, and Karen Yamamoto Hackler as June. PHOTO BY JAMES A. NAKAMOTO.

Aloha Las Vegas at the Japan America Theatre, 1994, directed by James A. Nakamoto, with setting modified from the original Kumu Kahua design by Joseph D. Dodd. The meeting between Alvin (Dann Seki) and June (Karen Yamamoto Hackler.) PHOTO BY JAMES A. NAKAMOTO.

Aloha Las Vegas, Pan Asian Repertory production, directed by Ron Nakahara, sets by Cornell Riggs, costumes by Hugh Hanson, New York, April 1998. The final family photograph, Act III. *Left to right:* Katsumi Nobori *(standing)* as Butch, Millie Chow as DeeDee, Ron Nakahara as Wally, Dawn Akiyama as June, Kati Kuroda as Gracie, and Paul Keoni Chun as Alvin. PHOTO BY CORKY LEE.

Production Credits

A'ala Park

The first full-length version of *A'ala Park* was produced by Kumu Kahua as part of the Studio Series at the Hawaii Performing Arts Company's Manoa Valley Theatre for a season beginning March 19, 1984.

Cast

OLDER MANNY Rodney Chang
AUNTY Marie Stires
BEAR Michael Afoa
CHAMP Shawn McKenzie
JEANIE Stacy Makishi
CABRAL Robert Ventura
MANNY Kevin Griffin
MAMA Jennifer Castillo
JOJO John Santiago
JIM Darick M. Ishihara
CAROL Susie Koshiyama
BILL John Rogers

Directed by Dando Kluever
Costumes by Phyllis Fukumitsu

The revised full-length version of *A'ala Park* was first produced by Kumu Kahua Theatre at its downtown theatre in the restored Kamehameha V Post Office, 46 Merchant Street, Honolulu, for a season beginning May 1, 1997.

Cast

OLDER MANNY Ray Bumatai

MANNY Warren Fabro

JOJO Kawika Allen

MAMA Laura Baring

BEAR Jarod Bailon

JEANIE Iwalani Campman

CHAMP Michael Ng

CABRAL Daryl Bonilla

SLICK Ron Serrao

UJI Larry Fukumoto

SWEENEY Steve Royal

Directed by James A. Nakamoto
Set Design by Alan Hunley
Costume Design by Lisa Omoto
Lighting Design by Gerald Kawaoka
Sound Design by Keith T. Kashiwada

Stew Rice

Stew Rice was first produced by Kumu Kahua at Kawaiahao Hall, Mid-Pacific Institute, Honolulu, for a season beginning May 7, 1987.

Cast

RUSSELL SHIMA Leighton Liu

ROLAND "ZIPPY" CHING Keith K. Kashiwada

BENJAMIN LEE Gary N. Nomura

SHARON Lei Kaniaupio

DONNA Stacey Makishi

RUBY Tammey Peltier

MISS FLETCHER Pamela Staats

Directed by Dando Kluever
Set Design by Joseph D. Dodd
Lighting Design by Paul Palmore

The revised, six-character version of *Stew Rice* was first produced by East West Players at 4424 Santa Monica Boulevard, Silver Lake, California, for a season beginning January 7, 1988.

Cast

RUSSELL SHIMA Keone Young
BENJAMIN LEE Marcus Mukai
ROLAND "ZIPPY" CHING Benjamin Lum
RUBY OGAWA Dian Kobayashi
SHARON UCHIDA Nancy Omi
DONNA WONG Karen Maruyama

Directed by Dana Lee
Sets by Yuki Nakamura
Lights by Rae Creevey

Aloha Las Vegas

Aloha Las Vegas was first produced by Kumu Kahua at Tenney Theatre, St. Andrew's Cathedral, Honolulu, for a season beginning September 18, 1992.

Cast

GRACIE Nan Asuncion
WALLY FUKUDA Larry Fukumoto
HARRY Dennis Ihara
JUNE FUKUDA Karen Yamamoto Hackler
ALVIN KAWABATA Dann Seki
BUTCH FUKUDA Byron J. Ono
DEEDEE FUKUDA Meredith Rose Hill

Directed by James A. Nakamoto
Set Design by Joseph D. Dodd
Lighting Design by Gerald Kawaoka
Costume Design by Trudi Vetter

Glossary

Carol Odo and Franklin S. Odo

Key

C	Chinese
F	Filipino
H	Hawaiian
HCE	Hawaiian Creole English
J	Japanese
P	Portuguese

aku (H)	skipjack tuna
akule (H)	mackeral scad
bafe (HCE)	bathe
bamboola (HCE)	big, hefty thing or person
bolohead (HCE)	bald-headed
brah (HCE)	brother
bumbai (HCE)	by and by, later; or else
buta kaukau	pig slop
char siu (C)	baked pork seasoned with sweet red sauce
chee	gee
daikon (J)	large, bulbous radish
hanabata (HCE)	nasal mucus
haole (H)	Caucasian, White
Hauoli Makahiki Hou (H)	Happy New Year
hybolic (HCE)	hyperintellectual
kahuna (H)	priest

kalua (H)	steamed in an underground oven
kapakahi (H)	crooked
kaukau	food; to eat
laulau (H)	food steamed in ti leaves
luau feet	wide, splayed-toed feet
li'dat (HCE)	like that
lōlō (H)	crazy
lōlō limu	dumb limu
lomi lomi	massage, mash
mahu (H)	male homosexual or transgender
make (H)	die, dead
malasada (P)	Portuguese doughnut
manapua (HCE)	Chinese pork bun
manini	small, tiny
manju (J)	Japanese pastry
Mele Kalikimaka (H)	Merry Christmas
Menehune (H)	legendary race of small people who worked at nights building roads, temples, and fish ponds
menpachi	red squirrel fish
miso (J)	fermented mung bean paste, used in sauces and soup
musubi (J)	rice ball
neva (HCE)	auxiliary verb indicating past-tense negative; "did not"
obake (J)	ghost
ogo	seaweed
'ōkole (H)	rear end
'ōno (H)	delicious
'opihi (H)	Hawaiian limpet, considered a delicacy
opu (H)	gut, stomach
pau (H)	finished
pilau (H)	smelly, dirty
pilikia (H)	trouble
pipi-kaula (H)	beef jerky
pohō (H)	waste

poi (H)	nutritious paste made by pounding cooked taro corms, served as starch
poi dog (HCE)	mongrel, favorite "breed" of local old-timers
puka (H)	hole
pupule (H)	crazy
saimin (HCE)	local noodle dish in hot broth
shaka (HCE)	sharp, terrific
sipa-sipa (F)	Filipino game
uji (HCE)	slimy, creepy
wahine (H)	female, woman

About the Author and Contributors

EDWARD SAKAMOTO was the 1997 recipient of the Hawai'i Award for Literature, the highest literary honor presented by the state. He has written fifteen plays, ten of which have Hawai'i themes. His plays have been staged in such places as Hawai'i, Los Angeles, New York City, San Francisco, Sacramento, and Stockton. He received Po'okela Awards for *Aloha Las Vegas* and *Our Hearts Were Touched With Fire,* and Hollywood Drama-Logue Critics Awards for *Chikamatsu's Forest* and *Stew Rice.* He has received a Rockefeller Foundation American Playwrights in Residence fellowship.

Mr. Sakamoto graduated from Iolani School in 1958 and received a B.A. degree in English at the University of Hawai'i in 1962. He worked for twenty years as a copy editor at the *Los Angeles Times* before retiring in 1995. He is a member of the Dramatists Guild.

DENNIS CARROLL (Introduction) is Professor of Theatre and Dance at the University of Hawai'i at Mānoa. He cofounded Kumu Kahua in 1971 and comanaged the theatre when these plays received their first performances. His books include *David Mamet* (Houndmills and London: Macmillan, 1987) and *Contemporary Australian Drama* (Sydney: Currency Press, 1995). He edited the anthology *Kumu Kahua Plays* (Honolulu: University of Hawai'i Press, 1983).

CAROL ODO (coauthor of Glossary), born in Honolulu, is a current Hawai'i resident and native speaker of pidgin/creole. She has a Ph.D. in Linguistics from the University of Hawai'i at Mānoa. Her 1975 dissertation is entitled "Variation and Change in Hawaiian English Phonology." She was responsible for the Glossary and standardized orthography of the 1983 anthology *Kumu Kahua Plays* (Honolulu: University of Hawai'i Press, 1983).

FRANKLIN S. ODO (coauthor of Glossary) is Counselor to the Provost at the Smithsonian Institution, directing the Office of Asian Pacific American Studies since 1997. He was chair of the Ethnic Studies Department at the University of Hawai'i at Mānoa and has been a Visiting Professor in Japan and at various universities, including Hunter College, Princeton, and Columbia. He wrote the foreword and glossary to Edward Sakamoto's earlier collection *Hawai'i No Ka Oi: The Kamiya Family Trilogy* (Honolulu: University of Hawai'i Press, 1995).